MY KI

The Reverend Margaret Cundiff was born in Somerset but has lived in the north of England since early childhood. Since 1973 she has served on the staff of St James' Church, Selby, in North Yorkshire, and was ordained deacon in 1987. She is also Broadcasting Officer for the diocese of York, Anglican Adviser to Yorkshire Television, and broadcasts frequently both locally and nationally. She is a regular contributor to BBC Radio 2's *Pause for Thought*, and to the British Forces Broadcasting Service's religious programmes.

My kind of day

MARGARET CUNDIFF

TRiANGLe

First published 1990
Triangle/SPCK
Holy Trinity Church
Marylebone Road
London NW1 4DU

Bible quotations marked GNB are from the *Good News Bible*, copyright
© American Bible Society, 1966, 1971, 1976, published by the Bible
Society/Collins, and are used by permission.

Bible quotations marked RSV are from the Revised Standard Version of
the Bible, copyright 1946, 1952, © 1957, 1971, 1973 by the Division of
Christian Education of the National Council of the Churches of Christ in
the USA, and are used by permission.

The song quoted on p. 118 from *Riding a Tune*, Stainer & Bell Ltd.,
1971.

British Library Cataloguing in Publication data

Cundiff, Margaret, *1932–*
My Kind of day
1. Church year – Devotional works
I. Title
242'.3

ISBN 0–281–04445 7

Typeset by Inforum Typesetting, Portsmouth
Printed in Great Britain by
BPCC Hazell Books
Aylesbury, Bucks, England
Member of BPCC Ltd.

Contents

Preface

When my family come home to find me busy in the kitchen, or maybe typing away in my office, or even with my feet up watching television, the first thing they ask is, 'What sort of day have you had?' As I turn my key in the front door, sometimes very late after a long day, my husband Peter rushes to meet me with, 'Had a good day?' Sharing the events of the day is part of our life. We are all interested in each other's doings. We get great pleasure out of sharing the delightful and amusing things that have happened. We also share the things that didn't go according to plan – the frustrations, the worries and the snags. By sharing our experiences, good and bad, we can help one another, give encouragement and comfort, spark each other off, and see the funny side of life – to be able to laugh at ourselves helps enormously.

I have a wonderfully varied life, and although it has a sort of routine to it, it is all very flexible. The very nature of my various jobs means that it *has* to be flexible. I have to be ready 'at the drop of a hat' to change my pattern. Yet thankfully it does all slot into place, and with a little juggling everything necessary seems to get done in the end, whether at home or away.

This book is about 'my kind of day', and the people and situations I meet. Not only my day-to-day life, but the pattern of the seasons, both natural and liturgical, both the fixed dates and the variety which arises from the needs, demands and opportunities of each day. At the heart of it all, the hub of my life, is my relationship with God. It is he who makes sense of it all; he makes the good things even more delightful, and the knowledge of his presence and his love gets me through the rough patches. He is my beginning and my end, and I can rely on that fact one hundred per cent, because I have proved it over the years, and have no doubts about the future.

The book is dedicated to all those who make up 'my kind of day'. My family and friends. Those I meet at church, in school, at meetings, on public transport and up the aisles of the supermarket, in their homes and their work places. Those I meet through my broadcasting and writing, and the many who share with me 'their kind of day'.

Most of all to my Editor, Myrtle Powley, who introduced me to the wonderful world of Triangle Books, and has steered me through the writing of seven of them.

. . . And to you, the reader. Come and share with me, through these pages, my kind of day, my kind of people, and the person who makes sense of it all – my God, who I pray will be yours too.

Margaret Cundiff
Selby, North Yorkshire
July 1989

1
Perfect timing

For a number of years I worked as a personnel officer for a textile company. It was one of those old-style, family-based concerns which took more than an economic view of their employees. They looked after them and their families, almost literally from the cradle to the grave: we had baby shows, pensioners' parties, works outings – all sorts of social activities. I was very much involved in caring for the workers' welfare.

At that time, thirty years ago, there were many unmarried mothers, often very scared young girls, and we seemed to get a spate of them around March and October, coming into my office for help. The foremen used to shake their heads gravely and remark on the dangers of Christmas parties and works holidays – and I suppose they were right in many cases. So the tears would flow, and I would do my best to help the girls, visiting their families, liaising with the then-called 'Moral Welfare Worker' and generally helping them to make decisions about the future. Quite often their babies were placed for adoption, as families did not always want the stigma of a daughter having 'got herself into trouble'. Many and varied were the sad stories poured out in my office by weeping teenagers, and I must confess I often wept with them.

I sometimes think of those days when I read the account of the Annunciation, when the angel Gabriel appeared to Mary and told her she was to have a son. When Mary asked how this was to be, since she was unmarried, the angel told her 'The Holy Spirit will come upon you.' And Mary accepted his words, and the consequences. She even composed a song about it – we know it as the *Magnificat*.

Now I heard some very strange stories from frightened girls in my time; but never one like Mary's. They may have tried to pull the wool over my eyes with some of their tales,

1

but no one would have dared to have come up with the story Mary told. Nor would I have believed them! Angels are the last thing a twentieth-century girl would mention on finding herself pregnant. I believe Mary's story, though, every word. Amazing though it may seem to modern ears, I am convinced that it is absolutely true. All the same, I am sure Mary must have had problems. What did her mother say? Or their friends? There would be plenty of whispering, pointing fingers, dirty laughter. Hard enough to bear for an unmarried mum thirty years ago; ten thousand times more difficult in Mary's day.

If it was embarrassing to be a young girl with a baby on the way, it was almost as embarrassing for an older woman, 'long past it', finding herself pregnant. When I was in hospital having our daughter, there was a forty-seven-year-old grandmother who had just had another child. You could tell that she and her family felt uncomfortable about it, particularly her husband. He used to come in looking very sheepish, and obviously took a lot of stick from his workmates. Elizabeth, Mary's relative, was in this position, with a child conceived when she and her husband were both getting on in years.

Mary spent the first three months of her pregnancy with Elizabeth. Away from prying eyes and gossiping tongues, they shared their worries together, rejoiced together, prepared together. In due course they were both to delight in the birth of healthy sons, Jesus and John, and to take pride in them as they grew and developed from boyhood to manhood. They were both to experience sorrow and grief. Eventually John was beheaded in prison, and Jesus was crucified. Nothing to sing about then, was there? Yet the two sons were to influence and effect the salvation of the world. Their mothers would always be remembered with honour. But was that any help to them at the time?

Scripture points to the fact that they did rejoice in God's will for them. They did accept the price they had to pay. They did trust God for themselves and for their sons, witnessing to God's love and power.

When we consider the story of Mary and Elizabeth, from a

human point of view it all seems bad timing. Would it not have been better for Mary to have been older, more secure, before taking on the responsibility of being the mother of the Messiah? Surely easier for Elizabeth to have had her child some years earlier. That is the way we might have planned it – but then God knew what he was doing. History was, and is, in his hands.

Sometimes in my own life I find God's sense of timing a little strange, inconvenient and annoying – at the time! It is only as I look back that I can say, 'Praise the Lord', knowing that he got it just right. Hindsight is a wonderful thing, but trusting in advance is the real test of faith. Mary and Elizabeth showed the way of love and obedience; the way of praise, too. The record of their lives is a song of praise, a song we are invited to join in, at any time!

My soul magnifies the Lord
and my spirit rejoices in God my Saviour
for he has regarded the low estate of his handmaiden.
For behold, henceforth all generations shall call
    me blessed;
for he who is mighty has done great things for me,
and holy is his name. (Luke 1.46–9)

Father, thank you for the examples of trust and obedience you have given us in the lives of Mary and Elizabeth. Give me that same spirit of praise and acceptance in my life, that your perfect will may be worked out in loving service, and in joyful worship.

2

This you cannot destroy

In the centre of our town there is a beautiful garden. It is a
real credit to our Parks Department; all the year round there
is a wonderful display of flowers, shrubs, bushes and trees,
and even in winter there is something to give pleasure. I
especially enjoy the spring, when the trees are heavy with
blossom and the fragrance beats all the expensive perfumes
that come out of bottles. The grass is neatly cut, and there are
seats where people can sit and talk, or just relax in the peace
and beauty of their surroundings.

But sadly, recently the gardens were vandalised – yet
again. Plants were ripped up, trees chopped down, and
although some can be replaced, trees don't grow overnight.
They will take years to mature – it's heartbreaking.

I know we are not alone in having to cope with this
problem of vandalism. Nothing seems to be sacred these
days, not even churches. Almost every day we hear of
churches broken into, objects stolen or destroyed, windows
and stained glass shattered.

Why is this, I wonder. What makes a person hit out at
beauty, destroy things that give pleasure – good things? So
often they are not stolen but just smashed – and left. What
advantage is there in doing that?

But there is a destructive force in all of us. I know I get the
urge, when I'm annoyed – and sometimes I give way to it – to
kick out; usually at the door, and I stub my toe, so I learn!
But some people seem hell-bent on destroying, hurting,
causing pain and grief to others. It makes me angry, very
angry. Why do they do it?

Not long ago a church in Hull was broken into for the
umpteenth time. Every cupboard was forced open and
drawers were pulled out. They had even used the cross from
the communion table as a battering ram to try to break into

4

the safe, twisting the arms of the cross in the attempt. Not being able to crack the safe, they had smashed some lovely leaded lights in their frustration.

The vicar, writing about the cross, said, 'Here I find a message. Do we judge them with condemnation or pity? With hatred or love? The open arms of the cross have both been bent forward, but isn't that what happened? Did Jesus not reach down to embrace each one of us? Perhaps that twisted cross speaks of the Christ who longs to embrace each one of those who showed no thought for him.'

I rang the vicar, touched by what he had written, and he told me, 'We've learned to live with it, Margaret. Hatred and anger are no answer. We want to keep that cross as it is, bent and twisted, to remind us of the love of Jesus for bent and twisted people – for all of us.'

That vicar is right. Hatred and anger are no answer. We have got to go on replanting flowers, and people; cultivating the beautiul, providing lovely things and places, in the hope that they will bear fruit, and in some way affect the lives of those around.

It is hard going, though. Sometimes it is almost imposs-ible. But then, God is the God of the impossible. He does bring good out of evil, life out of death, sense out of non-sense. And he asks us to be partners with him in doing it.

When they came to the place which is called The Skull, there they crucified him, and the criminals, one on the right and one on the left. And Jesus said, 'Father, forgive them, for they know not what they do.' (Luke 23.33–4 RSV)

Lord Jesus,
if you could love and forgive
    so much,
help me to love and forgive
    as well.

3
Come and join us

I once found myself mixed up in a demonstration – and it wasn't very pleasant. In fact it was quite frightening.

I had been invited to a dinner, and having parked my car, was making my way to the public building where the function was to take place. As I drew near, I heard shouting and found my way blocked by a crowd of people, chanting and carrying banners. I decided to take another route, but found that the crowd was standing outside the building where I was to go. They were demonstrating against the person who was to be the main speaker.

I stood nervously on the edge of the crowd, wondering how I could get through. I had almost decided to go home rather than cross the road when a friendly policeman saw my problem. He pushed his way through the mob and assisted me – or rather I clung on to him – and quickly got me through the entrance.

All through the dinner the demonstrators could be heard, and it rather took the edge off my enjoyment of the evening. But fortunately, by the time we went home they had got tired of waiting and had gone away.

Crowds have an identity all of their own, and crowds are very fickle. If all goes well, they will cheer their heads off, but if things do not go their way, soon those same cheers will change to jeers and boos. Hell hath no fury like a crowd disappointed!

When Jesus rode into Jerusalem the crowds cheered him. They made a path for him, and threw down their clothes and their palm branches like a carpet. Here was their Saviour. Here was the one who would throw off their oppressors. Here was the one who would lead them to victory – NOW. 'Hosanna!' they shouted. 'Hosanna – Save NOW! – much as a modern crowd, cheering on their favourite team, would

6

shout, 'Easy! Easy!' Many of them would be unaware of what it was all about; they were there simply to witness a spectacle. Some of them, no doubt, were just 'in the way', as I was at that demonstration. Probably the same people would be 'in the way' a few days later, when the crowd shouted for the blood of Jesus – 'Crucify! Crucify!' It is a brave man or woman who will defy a crowd; it is much easier to go along with it. Crowds have a habit of getting nasty with someone who is out of tune with their cause.

Let's be honest – we all have a crowd mentality. We simply follow the others, often without much thought or reason. We would be wise to stand back and make up our own mind whether to go back, go with or go through. We must choose, and act, for ourselves.

Each year, in Holy Week, I am given a palm. It is not much use for waving about, or putting on the road. As a symbol, it is rather small and insignificant. It is twisted into the form of a cross, the sign of the one who saves now, the 'Son of God who loved me and gave himself for me'. I don't wave it about, but I do look at it, think about it, and thank the one who rode into Jerusalem as King for saving me. I ask him to keep me faithful whatever happens, however life changes. And I pray that I may be 'his faithful soldier and servant to the end of my life'.

When he came near Jerusalem, at the place where the road went down the Mount of Olives, the large crowd of his disciples began to thank God and praise him in loud voices for all the great things that they had seen: 'God bless the king who comes in the name of the Lord! Peace in heaven and glory to God!'

Then some of the Pharisees in the crowd spoke to Jesus. 'Teacher,' they said, 'command your disciples to be quiet!'

Jesus answered, 'I tell you that if they keep quiet, the stones themselves will start shouting.' (Luke 19.37–40 GNB)

Lord Jesus, you are King. You are reigning. You are seated at the right hand of God in glory. Come afresh into my life, and take control. Come with your gift of peace. Give me victory over those things which would take your place. Hosanna — save now.

4
The Lord is here!

When you are only five, and have not been at school long, life is very exciting and wonderful, but a bit confusing and frightening too. There is always something else to remember, new things you've got to do, and everybody is bigger than you. On Fridays, two grown-ups come to school. They are not teachers, but it is a sort of lesson, not in the classroom but in the hall. They tell you stories about God, and there are songs which you don't know but everybody else does, because they can read. And there are prayers, and you don't know all the words, but it's nice.

Then the grown-ups say that next week we will all be going to church, that big building next to the school, and you can bring your mum and dad, and anybody can come, not just those who go to the school. Then the teacher reminds you again that it is going to be a special service, because it is for Easter, and you know about Easter because you're getting some Easter eggs and you're going to have a holiday. She says the church is God's house, so you must be very good and learn your song properly. So it must be very special indeed. And if you are going to God's house, will he be there? You ask your teacher and she smiles and says she expects so. And next week when you go to church it is special, like they said, and God is there, and you tell your teacher, and she smiles again.

End of term for Wistow School. It was Maundy Thursday and we went into church for the service. The five-year-old did ask if God was coming, and he did, with great excitement, inform us that 'He's here!'

I wonder what, or who, that small boy did see? I would have loved to have asked him, but it was too precious to be questioned. He expected God to be there – after all, it was God's house. I could have explained that to him. But I still long to know how he *knew* God was there. Was it the vicar in

9

his robes? No, he knows that the vicar is the vicar. Was it someone's dad? Perhaps the one with the beard? No, he would have pointed at him. All he said was, 'He's here!'

During the service I told them the story of the Last Supper. I had my visual aids, a bowl and a towel, a small table with a cloth on it, a loaf, a bottle of wine. It was quite easy explaining about the bowl and the towel: 'What does your mum say before you have your tea?' All the hands shot up: 'Wash your hands.' And to my question, 'Why?' came the immediate answer in a broad Yorkshire accent: 'Because they're mucky.'

Easy then to explain about 'mucky feet', and about caring and sharing. Then I took the loaf and said, 'Jesus took the bread and said, "This is my body given for you; do this in remembrance of me." ' And as I broke the bread I looked at the church full of children, teachers, parents and friends, and there was silence; a very powerful silence, a holy silence. I could feel tears stinging my eyes, at the sight of those wide-eyed children who, perhaps for the first time in their lives, were hearing those words and seeing that action.

But there was more than that; more than concentrated attention. I cannot describe it, except to say that it was one of the most beautiful and moving moments of my life. But someone else's words describe it perfectly; the words of a five-year-old: 'He's here!'

Jesus called the children to him, and said, 'Let the children come to me and do not stop them, because the Kingdom of God belongs to such as these. Remember this. Whoever does not receive the Kingdom of God like a child will never enter it.' (Luke 18.16–17 GNB)

Lord, thank you that you reveal yourself not just to those who are clever, those who are good, those who understand, but to children, and to those who have the heart and mind of a child. Give me such a heart and mind, that I may know your presence in my life today.

5
Does it matter?

All over the world each year Christians join in celebrating the great central fact of their faith, the resurrection of Jesus Christ from the dead. The joyful acclamations ring out from tiny village chapels and great cathedrals, echoed by vast congregations or by individuals, perhaps isolated from any fellow-Christians, but who equally can say, 'Christ IS risen. He is risen indeed!'

For me Easter Day is the most exciting day of the year, even more so than Christmas. Perhaps this is partly because of the nature of the build-up over the weeks beforehand. The six weeks of Lent have given time for reflection, for thinking out again the faith which I profess to hold, looking at my lifestyle in the light of that faith, and trying by God's grace to turn words into deeds. Then we live through the drama of Holy Week, the awesomeness of Maundy Thursday, remembering how Jesus had that last supper with his friends, and said those words which we remember at every Holy Communion service: 'This is my body. This is my blood . . .' and the stark horror of the events of Good Friday – rejection, desertion, death, silence . . .

And then suddenly Easter Day bursts upon us, every year afresh as if for the first time. Oh yes, the hymns are the same each year, and the Bible readings, and the flowers and the decorations, but Easter Day is always a glorious surprise, with its good news of life after death. C.S. Lewis wrote of being 'surprised by joy'; and I suppose that is how it is for me. I'm surprised all over again by the joy of it all, the power of it all, the truth of it all. So for me everything does come to a head on Easter Day. What I know and believe every day has this special focus on this special day.

But when you think about it, the First Easter would not have been anything like our Easter celebrations. There were

11

no joyful shouts that morning, only sadness and despair and blind panic. From all the evidence of the past week, it would have seemed that there was no reason for hope at all. Jesus had been crucified. He had been buried. That was a fact, a very public fact. It must have seemed the end of the line for those who had trusted him and had been confident that he was going to win through in the end. There is not much you can do when all your hopes are dead and buried.

Then Mary goes to visit the grave, something bereaved people have always done, the loving respect paid to the dead from the living. But she is shocked to find the tomb empty. She runs to get help from two more of Jesus' friends, Peter and John, then, alone, she just stands there, broken-hearted . . . And then, as the light of Easter Day begins to dawn, Jesus appears to her, reassures her that he is alive, and tells her to go and share the good news. (But of course, they don't believe her – women get so over-excited!)

On the same day, two other friends of Jesus are walking sadly away from Jerusalem to their home at Emmaus, disappointed, puzzled, forlorn. And then a stranger walks with them, and he seems to be able to explain things to them. They ask him in for supper, and as they sit together over their meal, he breaks the bread, and they know who it is: Jesus, risen, alive . . . So they speed back to Jerusalem with the good news.

By now the message is beginning to get through. Others have seen Jesus as well, and have spoken with him. He comes into the room where they are gathered together; and although the absent member on that occasion, Thomas, can't accept their word for it, later on he, too, meets with the risen Jesus, and exclaims with joy and awe: 'My Lord and my God.' . . .

And so it goes on, Jesus revealing himself alive, to individuals, to groups small and large, to friends and believers, and then to those who, like Saul of Tarsus, were enemies and unbelievers. And so it has gone on, for nearly two thousand years.

Yes, there was *one* Easter Day, when Jesus rose from the dead. But every day is Easter Day as men and women come to experience for themselves the Risen Jesus in their lives. For me, that experience came in my late teens, but I recently met someone for whom it happened in her eighties. It can come at any age, at any time, and in any situation. Some people have met him in times of great joy and excitement, others when they have been desperately sad or lonely. For some it happened when they were frightened or ill, for others when life was great . . . What matters is not when and where, but that they met with him. Because each one will testify that for them life changed at that moment. They suddenly knew the joy of living, the assurance of a new life – for ever.

Does it matter if the Easter story is true or not? Of course it does. As St Paul put it:

> If Christ has not been raised from death, then we have nothing to preach and you have nothing to believe . . . But the truth is that Christ has been raised from death. (1 Corinthians 15.13,20 GNB)

I can't prove the truth of the resurrection to you, except to point you to the Scriptures, to the witness of the Church, to the testimony of men and women today, and to my own experience. And you are no different from anyone else. Jesus died for you, and rose again so that you might know the joy of new life. He offers his new life to you. He wants you to enjoy it – for ever.

> Very early on Sunday morning the women went to the tomb, carrying the spices they had prepared. They found the stone rolled away from the entrance to the tomb, so they went in; but they did not find the body of the Lord Jesus. They stood there puzzled about this, when suddenly two men in bright shining clothes stood by them. Full of fear, the women bowed down to the ground, as the men said to them, 'Why are you looking among the dead for one who is alive? He is not here; he has been raised.' (Luke 24.1–6 GNB)

Living Lord Jesus, you have conquered sin and death. Come among us in your risen power now, and make your presence known to us. Speak your message of peace and hope to our hearts, so that we may live your risen life for ever more.

6
In the post

I like getting letters – it is a good thing I do, because I get a lot, and most of them need answering. Some, of course, I throw straight into the bin, including all those circulars telling me how to borrow money, and even more telling me how I could spend all the money I borrowed. There is information from societies and organisations wanting my support, and from those I do support telling me the date of the next meeting, along with the minutes of the last committee.

But then there is the mail I really enjoy, personal mail from friends and family, and also from strangers who have written to me after hearing me broadcast or reading one of my books. That's great, because I've made so many new friends from all over the world, and I've never even met them, except through the radio or my writing – I find it very exciting to have all those pen friends.

Most letters I answer and then throw away, but some I keep, because they are special. I've got some which my children wrote when they were small, and those from my husband Peter – although he is not a great letter writer, he picks cards with just the right words! I've letters from my mum and dad – mainly from Mum. (Dad is no writer – why is it nearly always the women who write the letters in the family?) I have loving letters written to me by friends when I was going through a tough time, as when Peter was very ill; others congratulating me on something – joyful letters, particularly those I received when I was ordained. Then there are the fun letters and postcards describing events, people and places which my friends have shared with me, and the letters that make me laugh – the 'cheer up' letters.

I like getting letters from abroad. There is something very exciting about envelopes with foreign stamps (I give those to the children's stamp club at the village school), and looking at the postmarks of exotic-sounding places.

Around Easter time one year, letters arrived franked with the words 'Jesus is alive'. They made every envelope special, even those old circulars and committee minutes, because they reminded me of the glorious truth of Easter, for all time – that Jesus *is* alive – for ever. I don't have to write him letters and wait for replies. He is right here with me, all the time, as he is with you. So whether you are a good letter writer or not, it doesn't matter. You can have a chat with him any time – like now. Why not?

I am writing this to you so that you may know that you have eternal life – you that believe in the Son of God. We have courage in God's presence, because we are sure that he hears us if we ask him for anything that is according to his will. He hears us whenever we ask him; and since we know this is true, we know also that he gives us what we ask from him. (1 John 5.13–15 GNB)

Living Lord,
you are here,
you are always with me,
wherever I go,
whatever I do,
every moment
of every day.
Thank you,
my living Lord.

7
Just a minute

The London Marathon has become one of the great events of the year. To see so many people running through the streets of London, determined to complete the course, is an encouragement and a joy. Some, of course, run to get a prize, others to beat their previous record. Most are running to raise money for charity, and they add to the fun by dressing in all sorts of weird and wonderful costumes. Then there are the disabled and handicapped people who take part, proving that they too can make it, given the chance and some support and encouragement. Every finisher gets a medal, however long it takes, and that's great. They all deserve their medals; they are all sportsmen and sportswomen in the finest sense of the word.

The most moving sight was at the start of the 1989 Marathon – all those people, eager and ready to go, but standing quietly for one minute's silence before the race began, in memory of those who had died just days before in the dreadful accident at Hillsborough Football Stadium in Sheffield. What should have been an exciting and happy day, when Liverpool and Nottingham Forest played each other in the semi-final of the FA cup, had turned into a disaster, with nearly a hundred fans, most of them young people, crushed to death through overcrowding in the stands. The tragedy stunned the whole country. During the days that followed, many such periods of silence were observed, on football pitches, in churches, and on the streets. Crowds and individuals stopped everything for a minute, life came to a standstill just for a minute, in memory and for the sake of those who had died, and the injured and bereaved. Just for a minute, for those whose lives stopped at a little after three o'clock on Saturday, 15th April 1989.

Just a minute. A minute's silence and reflection amid all

the busyness and excitement and demands of life. Maybe it would be good if all of us took just one minute each day to stop, think and reflect on our own lives. To ask ourselves where we are going, what we are trying to achieve, what we are doing with the precious gift of life which we have been given. Just a minute to give God the chance to get through to us, to speak to us. Just a minute to bring other people into his presence. A minute to ask him for help and strength in our busy life. A minute to pray for peace in our world, our country, our homes and our hearts.

Just a minute. Not much to ask, is it? Not much to give. Yet if we did spend just a minute each day in silence, then maybe things would happen in our lives, in the life of the community, even in the world. Who knows what a difference a minute, your minute, might make? It doesn't sound much, but then a minute can make all the difference in any situation; so surely it can make a diference when it is spent in silence, just as much as when it is spent in activity. A minute's space between activities. A space to be, rather than to do. A space for God.

Like all other disasters, Hillsborough will gradually fade from memory, except for those personally involved. From time to time we will be reminded of it, at anniversaries, or in 'review of the years' programmes on radio and television. But in the main we will forget, and our lives will continue on their headlong, busy way.

Just a minute – what about it? A minute a day. Jesus, at the time of his greatest trial, in the Garden of Gethsemane, asked his friends very sadly, 'Could you not watch with me one hour?' They let him down. They lost their chance to share with him then. They lost out.

Just a minute. Could you give one minute out of all the minutes you have been given today?

Be still, and know that I am God. (Psalm 46.10 RSV)

Lord,
Help me to be quiet for a minute,
just a minute,
to know your presence
and your power.

8
Bridge that gap!

The town where I live is famous for two things – its beautiful
Norman abbey and its ancient toll bridge. Selby itself stands
on a bend of the river Ouse. Though it is many miles from the
sea, ships are still built here, and launched regularly –
sideways; the river isn't wide enough to launch them the
more traditional way. It is a busy river. Ships go up and down
– and so does the toll bridge; and when it does go up, several
times a day, then the whole town comes to a standstill. We are
'bridged', and unless we make a long detour across country
and over another bridge, then we have to sit and wait.

I have spent many hours in my car, within sight of home, at
the wrong side of the bridge, and there was nothing I could
do about it. Like all the other motorists I moan and fume, but
the bridge has the last say. Letters are written to the papers,
even the Queen has been petitioned, and the Council mem-
bers have sat through many a long and wearying session
debating our need for a bypass, but we still have the bridge.

It struck me recently, though, sitting in the queue of
traffic, how fortunate we are to have a bridge. Where would
we be without it? We may grumble, but most of the time it is
effectively in operation.

There is something very beautiful about a bridge, be it the
Selby toll bridge, or a magnificent example of engineering
skill like the Humber bridge, or a simple rustic bridge over a
country stream. Thank God for the bridge builders. Yet as
we drive or walk over the results of their labours we probably
never give them a thought.

It is rather like that with the people who help us through
our lives, who stand by us through our disappointments, and
enable us to develop as people: our families and friends,
schoolteachers, ministers, those we meet every day in the
shops, at work, up the road. These are the people who make

life pleasant and easy through a word, a smile, a helping hand. We take them for granted, we may even grumble about them from time to time, but where would we be without them? They are the 'bridge builders', the ones who bother to make our lives easier because they care about us. Like bridges they come in all shapes and sizes, and all ages, ranging from the rustic to the magnificent, the ancient and the modern. Thank God for them, I say, and for all they mean to us.

Perhaps we could do our own bit of bridge building, say thank you to them and join them – because there is always a need for bridge builders, and bridge repairers. Bridges need to be kept in good repair, otherwise they are prone to cause an accident, or even a full-scale disaster. That goes for our relationships, too. Maybe a bit of routine maintenance wouldn't go amiss.

Help to carry one another's burdens, and in this way you will obey the law of Christ . . . So then, as often as we have the chance, we should do good to everyone, and especially to those who belong to our family in the faith. (Galatians 6.2,10 GNB)

Thank you, Father, for all those
    who make our passage through life easier
    by their love and concern for us.
May we be inspired to share
    in the work of healing and reconciliation,
    and be 'bridge builders'
    in our day and generation,
for Christ's sake.

9
The living proof

Did you know that the Queen sends out over 1700 tele-messages each year congratulating people who have reached their hundredth birthday? When she came to the throne in 1952 it was around two hundred a year – so there are nearly nine times as many now. And maybe there is a bulge of ninety-year-olds waiting for their turn! It does seem to point to the fact that people are living longer these days. In fact, a survey has recently been carried out for an official report on the subject, and yes, we are living longer.

How are we managing to do this? The report suggests three main reasons.

The first is a reduction in air pollution. Maybe that is so, but I can't help thinking we have just exchanged one sort of air pollution for another.

The second reason is better nutrition – in spite of all the complaints we hear about fast foods and fish and chips and takeaways!

And the third reason? The report says that 'the decline in belief in the afterlife may have increased the urge to stay alive in this one'.

Now I think that all of us, if we feel well enough to cope with living, want to stay alive as long as we can. I'd like to see my family settled, and maybe grandchildren growing up. There are things I want to do, places I want to see, work I'd like to finish, before I go. But I am looking forward to heaven – and I do believe there is such a place, and that it is a good place because it is the Kingdom of God, not of men.

Jesus promised that all who trust God and believe in him will go to heaven – and I trust his word one hundred per cent. In fact, I see this life and eternity as all bound up in one another, because after all, God is God of earth and heaven.

Yes, if I live to be one hundred – and I'll be an awkward old

soul by then, I expect – I shall enjoy getting my telegram
from the King or Queen of the day. But that will not be until
2032. In the meanwhile I'm enjoying this life very much – on
my way to heaven!

There are many rooms in my Father's house, and I am
going to prepare a place for you. I would not tell you
this if it were not so. And after I go and prepare a place
for you, I will come back and take you to myself, so that
you will be where I am. (John 14.1–3 GNB)

*Thank you, Lord, for all the joy of living, for all that
makes this world a good place to be in, for all those who
make me glad to be alive. Thank you that my future life is
even more wonderful than I could ever imagine, because my
future is with you – for ever.*

10
Today is the day!

Conferences, for me, are a way of life – and some are better
than others. I have my own special star-rating for them,
taking into consideration the various factors such as location,
food, company – and yes, I had better include subject matter
and speakers!

One 'gold star award' conference I attended was in Devon,
in a splendid elegant old house on the edge of Dartmoor. It
had everything – convenience, service, lovely surroundings,
good company and, the crowning glory, beautiful weather; a
perfect English spring.

On the last day of the conference we were asked to write a
contract with ourselves, saying what we planned to accom-
plish in our work during the next twelve months. This
contract was to be placed in a sealed, self-addressed envelope, and would be forwarded to us a year later; then we
could see how our agenda of hope had worked out.

It was a sensible idea, I suppose, an opportunity to ask
searching questions of ourselves, like 'What am I doing?',
'Why?', 'Where am I going?' It was a challenge to back up
our hopes and dreams with concrete application, converting
'I'm thinking about it' to 'I'm working on it.' As I sat staring
at my blank piece of paper, all sorts of wonderful schemes
raced round my mind; then, as I looked across the sunlit
garden and heard the birds singing their hearts out, I said to
myself firmly, 'Margaret, blow next year! Enjoy today, and
thank God for it!'

I'll be honest with you. I spent the time allocated for
writing that contract 'just sittin' ', and all I wrote was a short
note of thanksgiving, because I wanted to say thank you to
God and record the joy of that present moment. That session
was for me the high spot of the gold star conference.

A year later my letter arrived. I had almost forgotten about it, until there it was amongst my post on a not very bright morning – just one other uninteresting-looking brown envelope, in my rather untidy handwriting. I thought at first it was one of those 'money off' offers I had sent away for. But as soon as I opened it and saw my letter, I was transported back to that sunlit garden in Devon. This is what I read:

Dear Margaret,
The birds are singing, the sun is shining, it's beautiful. Look out in front of you at the flowers, the primroses on the banks. Think of yesterday, the walk along the river. Think of this afternoon, the sea! Think of friends, fun, love. Aren't you blessed? Think of all you have enjoyed. Give thanks to the Lord. Remember all the way he has brought you. Now go in peace, to love and serve the Lord.
Love from Margaret

I didn't get to the following conference, so I didn't have to give an account of myself. Maybe it was just as well. I couldn't gloat over minor triumphs or gloss over lost opportunities, I hadn't kept a record of them. But that letter has given me enormous pleasure, and will continue to do so. I have been able to take out that moment of joy like a precious jewel, hold it up to the light and see it sparkle, the brilliant colours leaping and chasing each other, then carefully put it away for another day.

Someone once wrote, 'God gave us memories so we might have roses in December', but we have to stop and enjoy the present moment, and let our memories take root in the fertile soil of the soul. I don't know how you are feeling right now, or what is happening in your life. You may be wishing you were somewhere else, doing something different, even being someone else, rather than you. But you are alive, and life is for living; so enjoy – yes, enjoy – today. It is God's gift to you. Make the most of it. And next week, next year – well, there is time enough for all that.

Live a day at a time, and start NOW.

This is the day which the Lord has made;
   let us rejoice and be glad in it. (Psalm 118.24 RSV)

Lord,
I am alive, this very minute,
and you are with me, right now.
That is all I need.
Thank you.

11
Don't just stand there . . .

It is said that if you want to draw a crowd, all you need to do is
to stand still and look intently up into the sky. In no time you
will have collected a group of people, all peering upwards,
looking for – well, who knows? – but determined not to miss
out on seeing whatever it is everybody else is looking at.

We all have a strong streak of curiosity within us. I know I
have; in fact perhaps too strong a streak – I don't like to miss
anything! If I saw a group of people staring upwards, I would
soon join them, wanting to know what they could see. I
wonder what I would have made of the ascension of Jesus?
One minute he was talking to his friends, the next he had
gone.

It was all very confusing for them, especially after the time
they had gone through. They had been following Jesus
around for several years, had the greatest confidence in him,
and everything seemed to be going well. Then it all turned
sour. Various people, including people in power, started
complaining about him, stirring up opposition. Then he was
arrested, given a mockery of a trial, and put to death. All
seemed lost, in spite of all the promises he had made.

Yet then the most amazing things happened. He re-
appeared, not just once or twice, but many times over a
period of forty days – to individuals, groups, large gather-
ings. It was like old times, nearly – but not quite, because he
kept talking about going away into heaven, and of how the
Holy Spirit would come and give them all the power they
needed to continue his work.

Then it happened! He talked with them, blessed them
and, well – he just went up! So they stood there, rooted to the
spot, looking, hoping he would come back. But he didn't.
After all the other exciting events of the past month or two it
was rather overwhelming. Then there were these other two

men they hadn't seen before, dressed in white, who asked them what they were doing standing there, and told them that Jesus would come back again, implying that they had better get on with doing what he had told them to do. So that is what they did. And although that was nearly two thousand years ago, and Jesus hasn't yet returned, the promise remains. Who knows when he will come back? But if he said he would, then he will. After all, he kept all his other promises; and if he could rise from the dead, then he can come back again any time, can't he?

Over the two thousand years since, people have taken that promise very seriously, and maybe some have made more of it than they should, making complicated calculations, using all sorts of methods, reading into Scripture things that were not intended, trying to work out when it will happen. Some of them have been made to look rather silly, too, announcing dates, and sitting on top of mountains, waiting . . . and waiting . . . and waiting.

But I suppose most of us don't give enough thought to the 'second coming'. We are too busy getting on with life to stand looking into the sky. There is no time to do that sort of thing, and not much point. Yet where is Jesus all this time? What is he doing, wherever he has gone?

The Apostles' Creed says that 'he ascended into heaven, and is seated at the right hand of the Father'. He has returned to where he came from, to the position of authority in glory. I suppose that is why artists depicting the ascended Jesus have shown him with a crown on his head, glowing with an unearthly radiance – a powerful sort of Jesus. For the past two thousand years his friends through the generations have gone on sharing the message, and the number of believers has gone on growing, and spreading, and waiting. Not standing looking up, doing nothing, but waiting in that positive sort of way, as when you are expecting someone important to call, and they haven't said when. It is a state of readiness, a pleasurable looking forward to what will be.

'He will come again . . .' It is something to keep in the forefront of our minds, an incentive to get on with the work he has given us to do and, as the Scouts' motto puts it, to 'Be prepared'.

We don't know when he will return: it cannot be worked out by any human calculation. But it will happen, of that I am sure. And when it does, I hope I won't be standing doing nothing, but enjoying the preparations for his coming; because it is going to be a great day, well worth waiting for. And well worth working for, too!

> For the Lord himself will descend from heaven with a cry of command, with the archangel's call, and with the sound of the trumpet of God . . . But as to the times and the seasons, you have no need to have anything written to you. For you yourselves know well that the day of the Lord will come like a thief in the night. (1 Thessalonians 4.16; 5.1–2 RSV)

> *Lord Jesus Christ,*
> *You triumphed over death,*
> *rose again, and ascended into heaven.*
> *When you return in glory,*
> *may I be found ready*
> *to welcome you,*
> *my Saviour and my King.*

12
Something to celebrate

With all the juggling around with our public holidays, we may have gained an extra day, but I feel deprived, because Whit Monday is no longer a day off. Whitsun, for anyone on the Lancashire side of the Pennines, used to mean 'Whit walks', when everybody took to the streets, either as walkers or watchers – the nearest thing, I suppose, to a carnival, in the best sense of the word. Bands and banners, and a 'bun fight' to follow, Whit Sunday and Whit Monday all seemed to roll into one, and the sun always managed to shine – most years! Whitsun meant new clothes, it meant flowers, it meant fun. Yes, fun! So what's wrong with fun? It's a pity we don't have more of it!

Now we have May Day and Spring Bank Holiday – but they are so tame compared with the Whit Mondays of yesteryear. I'm quite sure that if I started a 'bring back Whit Monday' campaign, I would have plenty of supporters. Maybe they would even bring out the bands and banners to help me.

With the loss of Whit Monday, Whit Sunday has almost disappeared from the minds of most people – certainly those outside the churches. It is just another Sunday, one nearer to the next holiday, the next opportunity to get to the coast, or to sit for hours in a tailback of other people waiting to get to the coast.

But all is not lost. Holiday or no holiday, Whit Sunday remains. Whit Sunday is for celebration, and not just inside the churches. It is for spilling out on to the streets, making a noise, getting excited, waving arms in the air, and being brave enough to tell people why. It is the celebration of the coming of the Holy Spirit in power on the Church – that first small group of followers of Jesus Christ. That power turned them from timid ordinary people into courageous sharers of the good news of Jesus Christ. The transformation must have been a shock to those who saw it happen; the only way they could explain it was to put it down to drink – it is surprising how brave some people can be when they have had a drink or two! Yet this wasn't due to drink – it was only nine o'clock in the morning, and your average drinker doesn't get too excited at that time of day. Those men and women were filled with something very powerful, and it was the power of God's Holy Spirit.

Power is a strange commodity. Most people want it, and many misuse it when they get it. To have power over others can lead to selfishness and greed. Power is easily abused, and the struggle for power, whether between nations, societies or individuals, can become a very dirty game. But God's power is a liberating power, not to grab from others, but to give. The Holy Spirit gives us courage and strength to do good, to share, to love. You don't have to fight for this power, either, but simply allow God to give it to you. Just one thing is required, you have to make space in your life for him; and that, for many people, is the stumbling point. They want God's power, but they want their own as well – and, like oil and water, the two can't mix.

In Selby, where I live, the Christians do take to the streets on Whit Sunday. From all the local churches and chapels they join together and walk through the town, with a band, singing as they go, praying, talking, rejoicing in the power of the Holy Spirit. They are an ordinary bunch of people, of all ages, but they know the power of the Holy Spirit in their lives, and they want to go out and share it with those they meet. Perhaps we don't have new clothes for the occasion – certainly not new shoes, old comfortable ones are far better on a walk – but we do share in a renewed joy in being together, celebrating together.

It is a pity we don't still get Whit Monday to continue the celebrations, but I tell you this; when we wake up on Whit Monday morning and have to get on with our daily lives, we don't wake up with a headache or a hangover. We wake up feeling fresh and free, because the Holy Spirit doesn't change. Even though Bank Holidays may change, he stays with us. We need his power on a wet Monday morning just as much as on a sunny Sunday afternoon, and God provides it, and will go on providing it, just as long as we will let him.

As for me, I know a good thing when I see it, and I know the difference the Holy Spirit makes. I may not understand it, but then I don't have to. I just say 'Thank you,' and 'Welcome!'

'When the Holy Spirit comes upon you,' Jesus told his disciples before he ascended to heaven, 'you will be filled with power, and you will be witnesses for me in Jerusalem, in all Judaea, and to the ends of the earth.' (Acts 1.8 GNB)

When the day of Pentecost came, all the believers were gathered together in one place. Suddenly there was a noise from the sky which sounded like a strong wind blowing, and it filled the whole house where they were sitting. Then they saw what looked like tongues of fire which spread out and touched each person there. They were all filled with the Holy Spirit . . . (Acts 2.1–4 GNB)

Holy Spirit of God,
come into my life
with your cleansing and renewing power.
Fill me with courage and joy
so that I may speak and share the
*   good news,*
whatever the day,
and wherever you put me.

13
Three in one

The phone rings, and the voice at the other end says, 'Could you come and speak at our meeting on . . .?' I consult my diary, and if the date is free say, 'Yes, I can do, but what do you want me to speak about?' There usually follows a silence, and then, 'Well . . . about your work.' My answer to that is, 'But which "hat" do you want me to wear?' There follows more lengthy discussion, until the theme is well and truly sorted out.

I must say I am not keen on those who ring me with such vague requests; it often means I am a 'programme filler', or they are not too sure of what they are about. I much prefer those who give a subject, showing that they have done their homework and are particularly interested in some topic they feel I might be able to help them with.

I do, though, give one talk entitled 'Many hats, one head' – which covers some of the various jobs I'm engaged in, and which people seem to find interesting, because for me variety is the spice of life, and I most certainly get variety! I am a wife and mother, and a deacon in the Church of England, which involves me in much pastoral, preaching and teaching work. There is the broadcasting, writing, and advising. I serve on various committees and councils, and as a selector for the Advisory Council for the Church's Ministry, which means meeting and interviewing candidates for the ministry, to help find the right way forward for them. Although I don't actually wear real hats – not very often, anyway – I do dress differently for my various roles. I don't wear my cassock in the garden, nor my old sandals and well-worn sun dress at council meetings in London; and my family tell me I have different voices for different occasions! I am still me, but I have different functions, and try to behave accordingly.

So in a way I have no problem when it comes to thinking of

the Holy Trinity – Father, Son and Holy Spirit – 'Three in one, and one in three'! I believe that God is one, and yet three, because I meet him in many ways. There is God the Father, the creator, the sustainer of the universe, my God. I stand in awe and wonder as I look at the world, at his creation, at the human and animal kingdoms. I marvel at God's dealings with his people in the Old Testament.

For me, it all became personal when I put my faith in Jesus Christ, the Son of God who came to this earth, suffered, died and rose again, at a known point in history, and yet is alive here and now. Jesus – God and man – who to the anxious pleadings of his friends, 'Show us the Father, and we shall be satisfied,' replied, 'He who has seen me, has seen the Father.' Who else could sustain such a claim but God himself? Who else could be encountered two thousand years after his death as personally as when he walked on earth in a part of the world now called the Middle East?

When it comes to the Holy Spirit, that, for many people, is the most difficult truth to understand. Father – yes. Son – yes. But who, what, is the Holy Spirit? I remember as a child being quite scared of this Holy Ghost I had heard about in church. I had a feeling of a something, a substance, drifting around, which I couldn't see or touch. It was all rather spooky, something completely outside my experience or imagination. Yet Jesus makes it quite clear, when he talks about the Holy Spirit as the helper, the comforter, the one who guides, that the Holy Spirit is a wonderful gift from God, the one who will enable us to know and understand the truth and give us the power to live it out. So if the Holy Spirit comes from God to help me, and he is just like Jesus, then I can know him personally. There is nothing vague about that.

People have tried to explain the Holy Trinity in all sorts of ways, making comparisons with a triangle, or a shamrock, which has three parts in one – but even then the Trinity is a glorious mystery. For me, that doesn't matter. I can delight to baptise 'in the name of the Father and of the Son, and of the Holy Spirit', I can pray for 'the blessing of God Almighty, Father, Son and Holy Spirit', because that is a reality in my life. After all, I, like most people, wear many hats, have many different functions, but I'm always me; people who meet me have no doubt about that, whatever hat, or outfit, or voice I have on!

I meet God personally as my creator, saviour and power. He is the one I know, and who knows me too. What more do I need this side of eternity? And then the whole truth will be revealed, and I won't need a triangle, a shamrock, or even a hat to understand it.

'I will ask the Father and He will give you another helper, who will stay with you for ever. He is the Spirit who reveals the truth about God. (John 14.16–17 GNB)

Almighty and everliving God,
Father, Son and Holy Spirit,
I praise you and bless you
for creating, restoring and empowering me.
Glorious and Holy Trinity,
I worship you.

14
Just one of the lads

It is a good few years now since I left my job as a personnel officer, but there are some people I met in the textile mills who I will always remember; there was something different about them, they stood out as special. Mike was one of these. He was a machine operator – 'semi-skilled' they called his job, but there was nothing semi-skilled about Mike. He was a real craftsman. He had worked at the mill ever since he left school, married a girl from the same mill, and they had two youngsters. He was a very proud husband and father, and loved to show me the latest pictures of his family, and tell me what they had been doing.

A good sort, was Mike. He played football for a local team, was quite handy with cars – the sort of chap who could coax a car into life even when you couldn't get more than a dull clank when you turned on the ignition. He was just as good with people. He seemed to be able to get that spark of life out of them, and got on with everybody. He had done the first aid course as well, in his own time; so cut finger or flat battery, Mike was your man – a reliable, cheerful sort, a 'salt-of-the-earth' type.

Mike was a Christian. He went to church, but never pushed it down your throat, it just came up naturally in conversation. He went on church camps and houseparties in the summer. They sounded like good holidays, lots of fun, and the photos he took showed a lively bunch of folk. He reckoned those holidays were better than Butlins, and in fact one year there was one of these church holidays at a holiday camp. They took the whole place over – swimming pool, entertainments and all. One or two of his mates said they wouldn't mind going with him some time, and he brought the brochures for those who were interested.

Mike didn't go on about his faith and church. He didn't set himself up to be different or, 'goody goody'. But he was

36

different. He was, yes, a good man. If you were in trouble, you knew where to go. Mike would listen, make a few comments, and they always helped you. He got teased now and again, and if he mentioned something about church, or some special 'do' he was going to, one of the lads would joke, 'Say one for me while you're there, Mike,' and he would smile and reply, 'Sure, I always do anyway.'

Mike was the only Christian I knew of in his department, but he never seemed to be in a minority. He had a quiet confidence, an air of security, and it rubbed off on others. They had confidence in him, and respected him.

'By their fruits you shall know them,' said Jesus. Mike, by his fruits, by what he was, showed who he belonged to. He was God's man. He was good at his job, too; he never did a shoddy piece of work, never nipped off early, and never took advantage of the boss being out. He didn't say anything to those who did, he just got on with his own work, and somehow that had an influence on the others. They looked a bit sheepish, a bit ashamed of themselves, even though Mike never said a word. Perhaps he didn't need to.

Mike showed by his life what he believed. Some people call it 'incarnational theology'. I call it being a living example. Mike was following in the footsteps of someone else who worked with his hands for a living, a carpenter by trade. He had the gift of creating something out of nothing, of mending broken things, and not just things, but people. You probably know who I mean – his name is Jesus.

When they saw the boldness of Peter and John, and perceived that they were uneducated, common men, they wondered; and they recognised that they had been with Jesus. (Acts 4.13 RSV)

Father
Thank you for those who in their daily work
show forth your glory,
who are not ashamed to be known as friends
of the Carpenter of Nazareth,
your Son, our Saviour, Jesus Christ.

15
Number, please

I dialled the number and waited as it rang out – it rang and rang and rang. Maybe I'd got a wrong number. I tried again. It just went on ringing. I asked the operator to try. 'Sorry, no reply.'

'But I know someone is there,' I protested. 'Could you check the number?'

A few minutes later the operator called back. 'The engineer has checked the line and there is nothing wrong. There's just no reply.'

I fumed and fretted, and then the phone rang. It was my friend.

'I've been trying to get you, but your number kept being engaged.'

'But I was ringing you at home, and you weren't there.'

'No, I had to go out. But as I had promised to speak to you this evening, I'm ringing you from a friend's house.'

Problem solved!

Sometimes when I pray I am tempted to think that God has forgotten me, or gone out, and that he can't, or worse still, won't, speak to me. I ask so nicely, but there is no reply. I plead, I argue my case, but there is no reply. I shout and sulk and, dare I say, sometimes threaten, but there is no reply.

It is not as though I'm being selfish. I want him to help the refugees, do something for those starving children, heal that young mother who is dying of cancer, ease the pain of the old man up the road. So why doesn't he answer? Why doesn't he do something?

Do you ever feel like that when you try to pray? Your prayers are ringing out, but all you get is the ringing sound coming back to you. There is no reply.

Maybe, of course, he is trying to get through to you.

Maybe if you would just wait and listen, then he could get through.

I'm not very good at waiting or listening; that's why I get myself into such a panic at times. I'm too used to getting automatic satisfaction – instant coffee, ready meals, quick cash points, push-button answers. But perhaps God works on a different system from me, a more personal one – and in his own time. Perhaps what he wants me to do is listen for a change. That way I might actually hear what he is saying, and learn to trust him, too.

> Have no anxiety about anything, but in everything by prayer and supplication with thanksgiving let your requests be made known to God. And the peace of God, which passes all understanding, will keep your hearts and your minds in Christ Jesus. (Philippians 4.6–7 RSV)

Father, sometimes I find it difficult to get through to you. So many other voices deafen me and distract my attenion away from you. Quieten my heart, and open my ear to your voice, so I may know it is you, and be at peace with the world, and myself.

16
Treasure trove

Our teapot has taken on a whole new interest since I read in the paper that a teapot which had been kept on top of a wardrobe wrapped in an old tablecloth, had fetched £14,300 in an auction at Sotheby's. It had been put on top of the wardrobe because it was too big to go on the kitchen table. The owner, a lady from Liverpool, was persuaded to put it in the auction by her sister-in-law, after discovering that the old, very impractical pot was Staffordshire creamware and might be valuable. To her surprise and delight it turned out to be worth even more than they imagined, and now she plans to buy her council house with the proceeds.

Well, our teapot isn't Staffordshire creamware from 1760 but stainless steel from 1960. It was given to us when we got married by some friends at work – they gave us the sugar basin, milk jug and hot water pot as well! We use our teapot every day. It's not beautiful, but it's useful; not valuable, but rich in memories. When I think of all those cups of tea it has held over almost thirty years, all the people who have drunk them – well, it's quite a treasure. It has sentimental value, you could say, rather than financial.

I suppose it is nice to discover a valuable treasure lying around the house. But for me the real treasures are the knicknacks which the children have bought us over the years, little ornaments my husband and I have gathered from holiday trips, family photos, cards and cuttings – tokens of love and friendship, holding happy memories; and when I look around at them, I realise how rich I am.

Have a look round you now, at your own treasures. Open up the memories, and count your blessings. Thank God for them – and enjoy your cup of tea, or whatever refreshment is to hand at the moment.

Cheers!

As for the rich in this world, charge them not to be haughty, nor to set their hope on uncertain riches but on God who richly furnishes us with everything to enjoy. (1 Timothy 6.17 RSV)

Thank you, Father,
for all your gifts:
the joys of each new day,
treasures to discover,
riches to share,
and love that lasts
for all eternity.

17
All good gifts around us

We once spent a holiday in the small town of Seefeld, in Austria. It was so beautiful, we didn't know where to look first. There were mountains all around us, and flowers everywhere. Every window, every corner, was ablaze with colour, and the air was fresh and clear. It was a wonderful holiday.

But you don't have to go to places like Austria to find beauty; it is around every corner. Even in the heart of a city there will be some oasis of green, a little park tucked away, a window box or a florist's shop window. Even on a drab cold day there is beauty to be seen in form and texture. See how the rain brings out colours, glistening on brick and stonework, how the sunshine lights up a dark corner or reflects on metal or glass. Even mist has its own gracefulness, with its delicate swirls, and snow has a purity and a whiteness that no soap powder or detergent can surpass.

Beauty, they say, is in the eye of the beholder. Perhaps that is true. Maybe we need to open our eyes and see for ourselves.

Jesus often pointed out the natural beauty of the world. He reminded people of the glory of creation, of God's care for the ordinary, the small, the unnoticed. The men and women around him were no different from us, being concerned with their own worries, their fears, their possessions or lack of them. Like many of us, they failed to see and enjoy what God had given them for free.

Here are some words of Jesus from the Sermon on the Mount:

> Look at the birds of the air; they neither sow nor reap nor gather into barns, and yet your heavenly Father feeds them. Are you not of more value than they? . . . Consider the lilies of the field, how they grow; they neither toil nor

spin; yet I tell you, even Solomon in all his glory was not arrayed like one of these. (Matthew 6.26–29 RSV)

I found on holiday, as I watched the birds in the woods, and the squirrels darting around our feet, the reminder I needed of God's wonderful provision. They certainly weren't worrying about food, they were just enjoying picking it up; and looking round the meadows I saw the most beautiful flowers, not cultivated at all, just common, ordinary wild flowers – but equal to anything in a fashionable florist's window. They were there for the looking.

Maybe that is the great value of a holiday; there is time to stop and stare, and enjoy what is there. Even God himself took a holiday, time off after creating the world. The book of Genesis says:

> God saw everything that he had made, and behold, it was very good. And there was evening and there was morning, a sixth day. Thus the heavens and the earth were finished, and all the host of them. And on the seventh day God finished his work which he had done, and he rested on the seventh day . . . So God blessed the seventh day and hallowed it, because on it God rested from all his work which he had done in creation. (Genesis 1.31–2.3 RSV)

One day in seven – a sit-back-and-enjoy-the-world-day. That is a good balance. All right, we probably can't always have Sunday off – we may have to work shifts – but we still need to have a regular day of rest and re-creation. Although I am terribly bad myself at taking time off, I know I feel the value of it when I do, and life is much better all round when I take time to discover and enjoy God's creation. It somehow puts everything into the right perspective.

But of course, it is not just things and places that remind us of God. God's greatest act of creation was in creating mankind – people. I like the description in Genesis: 'The Lord God formed man of dust from the ground, and breathed into his nostrils the breath of life; and man became a living being' (Genesis 2.7). The breath of life! God's breath. We are made in the image of God; there is something of God in all of us, and in everybody.

I recognise God in people often. I see something of his beauty and goodness and creativity. I experience his love and care and forgiveness through other people. Sometimes it is hard to see God when people are difficult or rude – the 'awkward squad' – and yet he is there in them, too, if we will look.

Mother Teresa and her Sisters care for the dying and destitute in the streets of Calcutta, and the reason they can do that work is that they see God in each person, however dirty, whatever is wrong with them, wherever they have come from; and they give them the love and care and respect they would give to God himself.

I suppose that is the secret, seeing others as made in the image of God. My vicar, David, often says, 'We are God's gift to each other, all of us.' When I look around sometimes, I think, 'What a gift! I'd rather have something else, thank you!' But David is right. God has given us himself, he has given us each other, and he gives us the grace to get on with loving and caring because he shows us what love and care is all about through Jesus. So let us thank God for his gifts to us.

Almighty God, we lift our hearts in thanksgiving for all your rich and varied gifts. For the life you have given us, for health of body and mind, for the beauty of the world around us, for the order and constancy of nature. For the loveliness of the changing seasons, for the fruits of the earth, for the joy of human friendship. And above all for the gift of new life through your Son, our Saviour, Jesus Christ.

18
What do I really need?

I confess I am a sucker for gadgets. It's all those glossy
booklets that keep dropping through the letterbox or out of
the Sunday supplements. They really are persuasive – I find
some of them quite irresistible. There are some amazing
things you can buy: gadgets that click on the lights, take your
blood pressure, record the impurities in the air, and all of
course stamped with your personal monogram – in gold!

But really, all these things are just toys, aren't they?
Expensive and sophisticated toys for adults. One I noticed
was described as 'another amusing piece of non-essential
gadgetry for the executive desk top' – well, at least they are
honest! But I bet they sell thousands, even to those of us who
have never had, or are likely to have, an executive desk.

These things are good for a laugh, but I sometimes fall for
them. I once received something I had ordered five months
previously. 'Great demand', they said, was the reason for the
delay; it seems that everybody, but everybody, wanted one.
It is a key ring that whistles, with a light and a digital clock on
it. The trouble is, it whistles at the wrong time; even the noise
from the fridge makes it howl. Then it doesn't answer when I
call it. Its clock is almost invisible and its light wouldn't
illuminate a pin head – so it is not really very useful at all. As I
said, I'm a sucker for glossy adverts.

That key ring was an impulse buy, something I didn't
need, and it doesn't work. All I need to do is remember where
I put my keys: 'Hang them up', as my husband is always
telling me. I could put a battery in the pocket torch I have had
for years; and if I really want to know the time, I have a
perfectly good watch. I don't need anything else, do I? The
plain and simple way makes more sense, is far more reliable,
and cheaper.

Perhaps that is a parable about life. If we stuck to old-

45

fashioned values like the Ten Commandments, if we followed the example of Jesus Christ and put honesty, courtesy and mutual respect back into fashion, then maybe we would all live a more satisfying life without the need for non-essential gadgetry.

As Jesus said, 'Life is more than food, and the body more than clothes.' Maybe he would have added today, 'more than whistling key rings'.

> You have been raised to life with Christ, so set your hearts on the things that are in heaven, where Christ sits on his throne at the right-hand side of God. Keep your minds fixed on things there, not on things here on earth. (Colossians 3.1–2 GNB)

> *Lord, help me to see what I really need,*
> *not merely what I want.*
> *Don't let me be so dazzled by the*
>   *baubles of this world,*
> *that I fail to recognise the treasure*
> *which lasts for all eternity.*

19
Love, love, love!

I was surrounded by flowers – roses, freesias, carnations, sweet peas. They were beside me, behind me, facing me. Some people were carrying them, others wearing them in their lapels or pinned to their dresses. I was at a wedding, of course.

It was a very special wedding, for me, because although I've assisted at quite a number of marriage services, this was the first I had conducted on my own. It had all the right ingredients – lovely bride, handsome bridegroom, dainty dresses, top hats and tails. The sun shone, the bells rang, the organ played, the soloist sang beautifully and the old village church seemed aglow with happiness too . . . And of course, there were flowers everywhere.

I was thrilled to be asked to conduct the service – delighted that Glen and Carolyn had wanted me to take part in this special day in their lives. Later, at the reception which, being a Yorkshire wedding, included roast beef and Yorkshire pudding, I said grace, thanking God for the wonderful day and for all his love.

A few days later, I was assisting at another wedding, in the south of England, when my nephew David married Gwen, so it was a rather romantic week for me.

But of course, there is more to marriage than romance. It is all about love – God's love and human love. The first sentence in our marriage service is: 'God is love, and those who live in love, live in God: and God lives in them.' The first question put to the bridegroom is, 'Will you take her to be your wife? Will you *love* her . . .?' and to the bride, 'Will you take him to be your husband? Will you *love* him . . .?'

Love is the key word, the essential ingredient, in any relationship, whether it be in marriage, parenthood, friendship, in the family, the community, or in the family of nations.

Love is very practical as well.

Just listen to these words of St Paul when he was writing to the Christians at Corinth:

'Love is patient and kind; love is not jealous or boastful; it is not arrogant or rude. Love does not insist on its own way; it is not irritable or resentful; it does not rejoice at wrong, but rejoices in the right. Love bears all things, believes all things, hopes all things, endures all things. Love never ends.' (1 Corinthians 13.4–8 RSV)

That is the 'nitty gritty' of loving; what it is all about. And looking at that list again, I know I fall a long way short of the mark. In fact, how dare I say I love anyone or anything? I dare not – me, Margaret Cundiff; but I have to go back to that opening sentence in the marriage service: 'God is love . . .' I've got to rely on him as my source of love, to let his love flow into me and out to others, even to those I find quite unlovely, or who are unloving towards me. Love is no easy thing, but it lasts, and anything that lasts is worth working for.

Love, they say, makes the world go round. So let us try a bit harder at sharing it. After all – all *you* need is love.

Father, thank you for the gift of love, that precious gift we can share with one another – husband, wife, parent, child, friend. May we never misuse or abuse your gift, but share it joyfully with one another – and with you.

20
Out of the ashes

York Minster had its night of sorrow, its ordeal by fire, on 9th July, 1984. I had been in the Minster attending a service the day before, enjoying, as I always do, being part of the worshipping community, delighting in the music, the splendour and magnificence of the building. On the following morning, I stood looking at a smouldering, blackened, wet mess. Firemen were still at work, workmen were salvaging what they could, and a crowd of onlookers watched silently, tearfully, from behind the cordoned-off area. Someone had placed bins with handwritten notices on them: 'For York Minster', and already people were emptying their pockets and throwing in what they had, to start off the restoration fund. Even before the fire was put out, the work of restoration had begun.

A little over four years later, the Queen came to share in a great service of thanksgiving to mark the completion of the restoration of the south transept. It was a truly wonderful occasion, greeted with joy, not just by the people of York but all over the world.

What happened to York Minster has been a marvellous visual aid. From death to resurrection. From sadness to joy. From despair to hope, and hope gloriously realised. It is a modern day parable of life itself. I know that in my own life there are times when all seems lost, when my plans have been dashed, cherished things destroyed. We all have our 'dust and ashes' days. As an old song puts it, 'Life is full of ups and downs' – and sometimes the downs seem very deep indeed!

Yet there is always hope – real hope, not wishful thinking. In John's Gospel, chapter 14, we have these words spoken by Jesus to his puzzled and anxious friends, just before he was arrested and condemned to death:

Let not your hearts be troubled; believe in God, believe
also in me . . . I will not leave you desolate; I will come to
you. A little while, and the world will see me no more, but
you will see me; because I live, you will live also. (John
14.1, 18–19 RSV)

The truth of those words was gloriously realised when
Jesus rose from the dead, and they have gone on bringing
hope and comfort to millions down the centuries. Against all
odds, Jesus rose from the dead. His life is experienced in the
world in spite of everything that has happened. His life is
seen in people, too, sometimes in the most unlikely people.
York Minster has been wonderfully restored, but that is
nothing to what God can do in human lives, for you and for
me. He can remake our lives, whatever sort of a mess we get
into, whatever the years have done to us. He has a plan for
each of us. But we have got to do our part, stepping out in
faith with him, co-operating with him as he remakes us,
makes us new people. The restoration of York Minster didn't
happen by magic but by hard work by many people, spurred
on by the God-given vision of what could be.
If you want to know more about visions, read parts of the
book of Revelation, the last book in the Bible. Perhaps it is
not the easiest book to understand, but in it we get a picture
of a new heaven and a new earth, based on the reality of God's
word. It is a picture of God's kingdom – and that, to my
mind, is a far more glorious prospect than a million York
Minsters put together.

Then I saw a new heaven and a new earth; for the first
heaven and the first earth had passed away, and the sea
was no more. And I saw the holy city, new Jerusalem,
coming down out of heaven from God, prepared as a
bride adorned for her husband; and I heard a loud voice
from the throne saying, 'Behold, the dwelling of God is
with men. He will dwell with them, and they shall be
his people, and God himself will be with them; he will

wipe away every tear from their eyes, and death shall be no more, neither shall there be mourning nor crying nor pain any more, for the former things have passed away.'

And he who sat upon the throne said, 'Behold, I make all things new.' (Revelation 21.1–5 RSV)

Open my eyes, Lord, to what you are doing
in the world,
bringing hope out of despair,
life out of death,
restoring and transforming human lives.
Give me a vision of what is possible
in your strength
of what is certain through your power,
not just in the future,
but today.

21
I remember . . .

The school was breaking up for the summer holidays. We had a
service in church in the morning, and parents and friends came
along to join in. It was a lovely way to round off the school year.
We thanked God for all we had enjoyed together, praying for
one another, and very specially for those who were leaving to go
up to secondary school in September.

It would be a big change for children who had spent all
their time up to now in a village school. I had a lump in my
throat as I looked at those eleven-year-olds. I'd known most
of them all their school life, and some even before – and here
they were, going out into a big, new world, away from the
village, for they were going to travel into town, whichever
secondary school they went on to.

During the week, they had written down their impressions
of their headmaster, Mr Thorne. Here are some of their
comments:

Mr Thorne has influenced my life, and I'll always look up
to him . . .

I would never have been able to get on with my life without
knowing the important things he has taught me, like how
to tie my shoe laces and put a chair under the table quietly.
He's showed me he is a man, not just a teacher . . .

Mr Thorne has taught me most of which I know, he always
handles things smooth, and has a way out dress sense. I
like the fun of hearing him sing on Thursdays . . .

Mr Thorne has taught me the very important steps of
dancing, I didn't know that you put your arms on the
shoulders of your partner, but I will always believe everything he says . . .

He has taught me NOT TO WASH papier maché models, especially snails. He has shown me how to mould clay into a ball, glue wood together and make buckets of paste, AND do neater handwriting . . .

– and maybe this comment says it all:

When he smiles he makes me feel like I have done something right for a change, and this makes me feel quite good. I like Mr Thorne a lot . . .

Children are frank, aren't they – and very observant.

During the service I talked to them about Joshua, who had the awesome task of following in Moses' footsteps, and about God's promise to him: 'Don't be afraid or discouraged, for I, the Lord your God, am with you wherever you go.' As I looked at those eager young faces, I wondered what life held in store for them. I expect they will many times be frightened, discouraged and tempted, but I pray that they will remember what they learned at Wistow School; what they learned of God in our assemblies together. And I hope that they will meet good people along the way, who will help and encourage them as Mr Thorne has done – and with a smile . . .

I know I have been talking about children, but we are all children, aren't we? And you may well be feeling a little afraid or discouraged. Maybe it is a fear of the unknown, or perhaps there is something looming ahead which you are not looking forward to, and you are wondering how it is going to turn out, and if you will be able to cope. Well, let me remind you of God's promise. It is for you – today – now. Hold on to it tightly, and let God hold on to you, too.

Don't be afraid or discouraged, for I, the Lord your God, am with you wherever you go. (Joshua 1.9 GNB)

*Thank you, Father, for all those who have
influenced my life for good:*

53

Parents, teachers, friends.
Thank you for memories,
for examples.
Thank you for your presence
which has surrounded me from the beginning,
and will until the end of time.

54

22
Food for thought

It has been said that most of the things which we enjoy in life are either immoral or fattening. Now it seems they are dangerous too.

Everything we eat seems to carry enormous health risks. No longer can we eat what our family calls 'dippy eggs' with 'soldiers' – fingers of bread and butter – making the perfect tea time combination. Soft-boiled eggs are definitely out, as are most cheeses, cooked meats, ready prepared salads, and a thousand and one other products, it seems. We are warned of the dire consequences of eating these things – perhaps even death. Soon we will not dare to enter the kitchen for fear something nasty may pop up.

Of course we need to take care over the things we eat, but maybe we are beginning to go overboard with caution. It seems to me that we have got things very much out of proportion when the greater part of the world has not even the basic necessities of life, yet we are trying to protect ourselves one hundred per cent.

If we took heed of all the warnings we would never eat anything, cross the road, or even open our eyes in the morning for fear of what might happen to us. In the Sermon on the Mount, Jesus told the crowd:

> I tell you not to be worried about the food and drink you need in order to stay alive, or about clothes for your body. After all, isn't life worth more than food? And isn't the body worth more than clothes? (Matthew 6.25 GNB)

I must admit I feel like that, too. If we would all get on with living, looking after one another, looking beyond 'us and ours' and giving a bit more thought to what God has to say about life, then maybe we would be a great deal happier and healthier.

What matters most is the sort of person we are, not the brands of food we buy, or the labels they carry listing the ingredients. Our eternal destiny is governed by our relationship with God and not by a government White Paper, not even one with green edges.

It is all a matter of assessing what really matters most to us, and where our deepest concerns lie; and working those out is much more important and far-reaching than any government health warning. Fashions and fads in food change, as do fashions in anything else in our changing society, but God's word remains – for ever – and never goes out of fashion.

As for us, our life is like grass.
We grow and flourish like a wild flower;
    then the wind blows on it, and it is gone –
    no one sees it again.
But for those who honour the Lord,
    his love lasts for ever,
and his goodness endures for all generations.
(Psalm 103.15–17 GNB)

Father, there are so many voices telling me what is good for me, and what could do me harm. I get so confused at times, so selfishly concerned for my own well-being. I forget that there is more to living than microwave 'know how' or calorie counts. Remind me afresh of your recipe for the good life, and help me to follow it faithfully.

23
The mountain top experience

'Come on, mum, let's go to Betty's for coffee. I'll treat you.'

I didn't need any persuading, and soon we were seated in a comfortable corner of that well-known York café, happily watching the world go by the window, enjoying our morning coffee. It was good being together, mother and daughter out on a shopping expedition. Alison had been home for a few days' holiday from London, where she works, and on this, her last day, we had decided on impulse to go into York and make the most of her last morning.

It was a perfect day. York was looking at its best in the sunshine, we had a lot of fun together, sharing as we do the same sense of humour, we were pleased with our purchases; and now, the final touch to a beautiful morning, coffee at Betty's. I looked at Alison, as I listened to her chatting away, and I wanted that moment to stay for ever. It was one of those magical moments of sheer happiness.

An ordinary thing, really, mother and daughter together, doing what so many mothers and daughters do together. No doubt there were plenty more around us in the café that morning. For me, though, it was such a perfect moment, I wanted to freeze it, press the pause button on life, and hold it there. I found it hard to release myself from it. But then I couldn't hold on to it, only in my memory, for life goes on, regardless of what is happening. Soon we were heading back home for a quick lunch and then off to the station for the London train. I waved goodbye until the train, with Alison on it, was out of sight. I stared at the track, then turned, blinking away the tears, walked back to my car and drove home. Back to normal, you could say; back to business again.

I think I can understand a little of how Peter, James and John felt when they experienced the transfiguration of Jesus up in the mountain. What had begun as an ordinary mountain walk with Jesus became something so special, so won-derful, that they wanted it to remain like that for ever. It was an ecstasy beyond their previous experience, a glorious moment; and having witnessed it and shared in it, they had no desire to go back down the mountain, to resume their everyday life. Down there were the problems to face, the demands, the fears and, looming in the distance, dark clouds of uncertainty. They had to go down and on, though. The moment of disclosure was over; but no one could ever take it from them, and later it would be recorded so that all of us could have a taste of what it was like, up on the mountain that special day.

'Mountain top experiences' – that is how we describe something extra special, our moments of great joy, exhilara-tion and glory. Some of these experiences are human – perhaps the wonder of birth, of falling in love, of shared pleasures, as mine with my daughter. Some are experiences of God, holy moments, beyond human making. Human and divine, secular and sacred – you cannot separate them really. They are bound together.

What has a moment in a York café to do with the Trans-figuration? I would say that the hand of God was in both, in different ways. The 'something' I experienced in my deepest feelings of love for my daughter, of knowing her love for me, was from God. I know it was from him because I caught a glimpse of his love in that moment – his love which binds us together; an assurance of his never-ending love, and his purpose for all his creation.

Peter, James and John caught a glimpse of that never-ending powerful love of God, that day on the mountain. They saw and heard God himself in it, and received a divine assurance that all was well; all was part of God's plan and purpose. Then, down to the workaday ordinariness of daily life. It was not easy, but life goes on; it has to, doesn't it? Life goes on, sustained by God's loving purpose and plan which will be fulfilled for each one of us.

After six days Jesus took with him Peter and James and John his brother, and led them up a high mountain apart. And he was transfigured before them, and his face shone like the sun, and his garments became white as light . . . and Peter said to Jesus, 'Lord, it is well that we are here.' (Matthew 17.1,2,4 RSV)

Almighty, loving Father, we praise you for the glimpses of glory, the revelations of love, you give us in our lives. May we not attempt to hang on to them selfishly, but allow them to release us for greater service in your world.

24
Come fly with me!

My favourite mode of travel is by air. There is something
exciting about airports, seeing planes taking off and landing,
and best of all, being 'up, up and away', getting to where I
want to be quickly and comfortably.

So, one rather hot Saturday in summer, my husband and I
found ourselves, along with thousands of others, at Manchester airport. We were waiting for a flight to Yugoslavia, ready
for our holiday in what was for us a new and undiscovered
part of the world. Inside the airport everybody seemed to be
carrying the world on their backs, and in their hands.
Hundreds of people were on the move, most of them going on
holiday like ourselves, but some on business; you could tell
them by their suits and briefcases, and their rather bored
expressions.

Our flight was delayed, fortunately for only a couple of
hours – some people had been waiting more than a day. After
yet another walk round the shops, and another cup of coffee,
I noticed opposite the restaurant a door marked 'Prayer
Room'. I walked across to it. A chorus of voices behind me
called out, 'Say one for us!' I assured them I would. Inside,
the room was cool, quiet and welcoming, simply furnished,
with Bibles in different languages and an invitation to sit, rest
and reflect. I caught sight of a small brass plaque on the wall.
It was a memorial to those who had lost their lives in a disaster
a few years ago at Manchester airport. They too had been
going on holiday, but they had never made it. Life for them
had ended on the runway, in a horrific fire.

Suddenly, flying took on a different meaning. The carefree
holiday feeling was slightly overshadowed by a tiny suspicion
of anxiety in the pit of my stomach. A verse from Psalm 139
came into my mind:

> Where could I go to escape from you?
> Where could I get away from your presence?
> If I went up to heaven, you would be there . . .

I had no need to be afraid. God was there, on the ground and in the air, and wherever I might go. Did it matter in the long run whether I went up or stayed down? All that mattered for me was to know the presence of the Lord in that moment – and I did. I did say a prayer, for us all – for myself, my fellow passengers and the pilot. I thanked God for family and friends, for the joy of holiday, the opportunity to see and experience new things and new places; but above all for his love which holds all things together – all time, all places, all people.

'Did you say one for us, then?' greeted me as I came out of the Prayer Room. I assured them I had, but added, 'Why don't you say one for yourself? You've got time.' My suggestion was not taken up – not that I could see, anyway.

Soon we were flying high above the clouds, over the sea, then landing most smoothly at our holiday destination, gathered up into waiting coaches and deposited at our hotel. It was late, very late, when I stepped out on to the balcony, listening to the lapping of the waves below. Up in the sky a thousand stars twinkled, and away in the distance a plane soared high, heading for another airport, another country.

Another day over, another flight, and now the bliss of head on pillow and sleep, body winding down, relaxing, stretching out in the cool darkness.

'Where could I get away from your presence . . .?' Nowhere – never.

'Thank you, Lord,' I said, 'and goodnight.'

> If I take the wings of the morning
> and dwell in the uttermost parts of the sea,
> even there thy hand shall lead me
> and thy right hand shall hold me.

If I say, 'Let only darkness cover me,
    and the light about me be night,'
even the darkness is not dark to thee,
    the night is bright as the day;
        for darkness is as light with thee . . .
    When I awake, I am still with thee.
(Psalm 139.9–12,18 RSV)

Father,
Wherever I am, you are there,
wherever I go, you are there,
wherever I will be, you are there.
Above, below, in the dark and the light,
you are there,
right now, here with me.
Thank you.

25
Why did Jesus come?

It was a very splendid service in Westminster Abbey. The Queen was there, the archbishops and bishops, clergy and lay people, all in their best attire. The music was magnificent and everything went off beautifully, as these things usually do. As I sat there feeling rather uncomfortable in a hat, I suddenly remembered a very different occasion. It was during the miners' strike, and I was talking to some pickets outside one of the mines in the Selby area. 'Whose side do you reckon God is on?' one of them asked me – and before I could say anything another young miner replied, 'If Jesus Christ was here today, he'd be with us on this picket line. That's why he came, to stick up for the oppressed. It says so in the Bible.'

Strange that I should remember that conversation while attending a festive service in Westminster Abbey!

Well, why did Jesus Christ come? Was it to be the focal point of grand occasions for the 'hat and gloves brigade'? Or was it, as the young miner said, to stick up for the oppressed, which he saw himself as part of on that bitterly cold day outside the colliery gates? And anyway, who was, or is, Jesus Christ? Where did he come from? What did he do? And what has it to do with me or you?

Perhaps the verse in the Bible which best answers those questions is in John's Gospel, chapter 3, verse 16: 'For God so loved the world that he gave his only Son, that whoever believes in him should not perish but have eternal life.' God's only Son! Quite a statement, that. Not just a prophet, a teacher, or even a miracle worker, but God's only Son. Not one of any number of sons of God, but the only one – a very exclusive claim indeed. If he was that, then we should take notice of him, and have a good look at what he said and did.

When he was here on earth, the Bible tells us, he went

round preaching and teaching and healing. Now the world has never been short of preachers and teachers, but Jesus was different. He claimed to be God, and to be the way to God. He didn't do away with the religious laws, but breathed new life into them. He introduced a totally new dimension into life, that of love for God and for our neighbour. He claimed to be able to forgive sins, to set men and women free to be new people, with a new power for living.

Yes, Jesus was a preacher and a teacher, but he wasn't all words, by any means. He healed the sick – many chronically sick, like lepers, the blind, the lame, those with mental disorders. He even raised the dead, and no one else had done that. He was called 'Saviour'. He saved people from their sickness, their despair, their frustrations, their prejudices, their sin, and from death. He saved them from themselves, and gave them a dignity, a purpose, and an identity. And for doing that, although some stood by him, in the main people rejected him, turned against him, and were glad to see the back of him. He was too dangerous to be allowed to carry on teaching, preaching and healing. He disturbed people.

Well, you know what did happen – a rushed trial, on trumped-up charges, and he was nailed on a cross as a common criminal – with two others for company, one on each side.

It could have been so different if only he had watched his words, had chosen his friends more carefully, had not made such outrageous claims, and had cut out some of the more sensational healings and raising people from the dead – he could have had a very successful career.

Yet how do you measure success?

He said all along that he would die. He also said that he would rise from the dead. He proved his promise. He did rise from the dead. So then his mission, his whole life, was a success. It did follow a plan – God's plan.

God so loved the world . . . the world of people, including people who occupy high office, like those in Westminster Abbey; and people who feel oppressed, like my friends on the picket line; and youngsters unable to find a job, who kick against society in their frustration; and the government minister who resigns his office over a principle; the world of people you and I are part of. God loves you and he loves me, and that is why Jesus came – to bring his love into our lives, to give us a new start, new hope for tomorrow, light on our way.

Jesus said this: 'I am the light of the world; he who follows me will not walk in darkness but will have the light of life.' (John 8.12 RSV)

I need light to see my way tomorrow, to sort my life out day by day, to get me through. That is why Jesus came, so I'm taking him at his word and asking for his help and his light.

I have come in order that you might have life – life in all its fullness. (John 10.10 GNB)

Lord Jesus Christ,
You came as the light of the world.
Be my light, show me the way.
Come with me, be with me,
now and for ever more.

26
Putting the record straight

In the year 1915, a lad called Harry won a medal as the top academic prize at his school in New Zealand. Seventy-four years later, Harry returned that medal to his school.

The reason? Harry had had a troubled conscience all those years, because he knew he didn't deserve the medal; he hadn't really won it. Harry was good at most subjects at school, but not so good at mental arithmetic, which was part of the examination. His seat mate helped him out with the answers, so enabling Harry to win. After all the years of that fact bothering him, he finally plucked up courage and returned the medal, telling his old school the true story.

When asked why he had bothered after such a long time, Harry said, 'I have got to make things straight before I push off.'

I'm glad he did so; now he can feel free. But what a pity he waited so long! He could have had peace of mind years ago, instead of waiting until he was eighty-seven – but better late than never!

Not so long ago a friend returned a book of mine which she had borrowed forty years before. I had forgotten all about it in fact, although I recognised it when I saw it again; the years rolled away. My friend said it was a relief to her to send it back. She wanted to put the record straight. Just like Harry and the medal.

When we think of the state of the world, and all the terrible things that go on, what do a medal or a book matter? Nothing at all – but to those who carry a burden of guilt, there is an anxiety which clings to them.

I wonder if you have something stored away that you should have unloaded. I don't just mean a medal or a book, or someone's silver spoon, or even a hotel ash tray – although if you have these things you ought to return them. No, I am thinking that maybe you owe someone an apology, perhaps an explanation of something that happened years ago but still troubles you, nagging away inside. Is there a letter you ought to write, a phone call you should make, someone you should visit? Take courage, say you are sorry. Make up that friendship. Write that letter. Pick up the phone. Call round. I know it is hard to do, but think of old Harry. If he could put things right after seventy-four years, then couldn't you?

I was talking about this to my husband Peter, and he commented, 'It could cause more trouble than it's worth. It would perhaps hurt someone to have the past dragged up; maybe they would rather forget.' That is something we have to face up to, but I do believe that 'where there's a will, there's a way' – a positive and loving way of going about things. I believe that God honours the honest action, and will bring healing and peace – on both sides.

A good prayer is that of the psalmist, who said:

Examine me, O God, and know my mind;
   test me, and discover my thoughts.
Find out if there is any evil in me
   and guide me in the everlasting way. (Psalm 139.23–4
GNB)

Lord,
Show me what I ought to do,
and give me strength and the
   love to do it.

27
Who knows best?

I was spending a few days in the Yorkshire Dales, at a Christian holiday centre. Also staying there at the time were forty children, nine- to eleven-year-olds, from a school in London, in the heart of one of the inner city areas. They were a great bunch of youngsters.

The weather was not all that good – in fact it was pretty awful, with rain and mist – and when the time came for the children to have their last full day out, walking along the river and up through the woods, I prayed that it would be a warm, dry, sunny day for them, so they would see the Dales at their best and have something to remember – maybe to encourage them to come back. But it only rained even harder. I felt so disappointed for them, especially as they returned from their walk soaked to the skin and covered in mud; but still full of fun and excitement.

'What an awful day you've had,' I said to one of the teachers who was peeling himself out of his wet clothes.

He smiled at me, looking quite surprised. 'Not at all,' he said. 'It's been a wonderful day. They'll never forget being able to paddle through streams, squelch through mud, and see the waterfalls cascading down the hills. Don't forget, they'd never have the chance to do that in London.'

Of course – I'd never thought of that!

Have you ever prayed very hard for something, or for someone, and God hasn't seemed to take any notice? Maybe the very opposite has happened from what you had hoped. Could it be that God had something better for you?

Forty London schoolchildren gave me cause to consider, that wet day in the Yorkshire Dales.

Truly God has listened;
    he has given heed to the voice of my prayer . . .
Blessed be God,
    because he has not rejected my prayer
    or removed his steadfast love from me!
(Psalm 66.19,20 RSV)

Thank you, Father, for reminding me
that joy can be experienced
in the storms of life,
as well as in sunshine,
and your love reaches beyond
my imagining.

28

A family matter

Our neighbours had been having their house painted, and Fran, the wife, popped round to tell us they had discovered some rotten wood that would have to be replaced before the painter could get on with the work. The TV news was on, and there on the screen we saw the effects of a typhoon in the Philippines.

We stopped talking and watched the dreadful scenes of destruction: people struggling for their lives, houses flattened, crops ruined. Then Fran said thoughtfully, 'It makes our bit of wood seem very unimportant, doesn't it?'

Just lately the world news seems to have been all of disasters, gloom and doom, droughts, floods, tornadoes, hurricanes and famine, so that I have a problem relating to it all. I'm almost punch drunk with it – one tragedy after another. The danger is that I will turn off – and I don't mean turn the TV off, but my head and my heart. It is all so upsetting, but after all, what can I do?

Yet we are one world – a global village is how it has been described – and we are one family, whatever the colour of our skin. Blood is all the same colour in any vein; tears are the same in every language.

Then I read these words – and they pulled me up sharply: 'The world is given to all, and not only to the rich.' Not words spoken by a politician or preacher looking at today's situation, but by St Ambrose, 1500 years ago. He practised what he preached, too, because his first act on being made Bishop of Milan was to distribute his wealth to the poor.

Feeling sorry for other people won't help them. It is only when it is translated into practical action that it is of any use. When you and I stop staring and start sharing – we could help each other if we really wanted to, couldn't we?

If a brother or sister is ill-clad and in lack of daily food, and one of you says to them, 'Go in peace, be warmed, be filled,' without giving them the things needed for the body, what does it profit? So faith by itself, if it has no works, is dead. (James 2.15–17 RSV)

Lord,
May my faith be a living and active faith
which shows itself in practical and generous
    concern for others.
Thank you for the privilege you give me
in allowing me to be an agent of your love,
sharing your resources in the world
    of today.

29
In it together

'One is one and all alone, and evermore shall be so.'

The words are from the song 'Green grow the rushes-O', and maybe you feel just like that – the lone Christian in your situation, family, workplace, school, neighbourhood – and it looks like it will be that way for ever.

It's tough, depressing and frightening at times. Sometimes you may think that it is not worth carrying on; that it is easier to be like the rest, or to keep your faith to yourself, to put it away in the box marked Private, and turn the key. If so, you are not on your own in feeling like that. Even some of the greatest servants of God have felt totally alone. Elijah the prophet ran away into the desert and wanted to die, and when God asked him what he thought he was doing, he said, 'Take away my life, I might as well be dead. I am the only one left.' God didn't argue with him. He provided food and water for him, and then when the prophet got his strength back reminded him very firmly that there were thousands like him, plenty of others who belonged to God and were trying to serve him, and that there was work to be done. Elijah was refreshed in body and in spirit, and then sent out to get on with the job.

On a 'wayside pulpit' many years ago, I saw the words, 'When you feel alone, remember, one plus God is always a majority.' I like that. It means that there is no such thing as the lone Christian; it may feel like it, often, but it just isn't true!

So the first thing to do is to thank God for his presence with you, for the gift of his Son Jesus who died for you, and for the power of the Holy Spirit within you. Stop reading for a minute, and start praising! It does work. I know, for it is something I practise when I am having one of my 'feeling sorry for myself' moments.

Look away from yourself, and look to God. What have you to thank him for right now?

The first thing is that he is there. He is listening. You matter to him. He is your Father, you are part of his family.

Then think about Jesus, about his life, his death and his resurrection. Read through some of his promises. Hear him speaking to you, promising you these things, and take them thankfully from his hands. Remember what he said as he was about to leave his friends: 'The helper will come – the Spirit, who reveals the truth about God and who comes from the Father. I will send him to you from the Father, and he will speak about me.' (John 15.26 GNB)

Alone? How can you be alone? Let this promise sink into your mind and heart now. Relax in the joy of it. Receive the assurance of God personally. It is for you, now.

Fear not, for I am with you,
    be not dismayed, for I am your God;
I will strengthen you, I will help you,
    I will uphold you with my victorious right hand.
(Isaiah 41.10 RSV)

Thank you, Lord, that I am never alone.
Help me to remember this even when I feel I am on my
    own.
Remind me of your power, your love.
Fill me with your presence,
Father, Son and Holy Spirit.

30
Come, ye thankful people!

Autumn – the 'season of mellow fruitfulness'. The turning leaves, from green to gold and red, the rich colours of field and garden. The shortening days, often lit up by a bonus of warm sunshine. And everywhere the harvest being gathered in 'ere the winter storms begin'. I've been busy freezing runner beans, stewing fruit and making jam, something I enjoy doing at this time of year. There is something very satisfying about bringing in the fresh vegetables and fruit from the garden and preparing them for the freezer and store cupboard. It's the squirrel instinct in me – 'good house-keeping' and all that. This is what has been flippantly described as 'holy marrow-tide', in other words, Harvest Thanksgiving.

Every church and chapel advertises its services, harvest suppers and celebrations. The children take their special baskets of produce to school and sing harvest songs and hymns, and preachers and after-dinner speakers are much in demand. Although I sometimes groan to myself as I look in my diary and see yet another Harvest Festival to preach at, I admit I do enjoy them. They are such cheerful services, and always attract good congregations, even people who don't normally go to church.

Walking into a Harvest service is like entering a cross between a Flower Festival and a Produce Show. Every available nook and cranny has its display, while sheaves of corn fill the porch, the choir have to climb over the sacks of potatoes and carrots, and the preacher fights through the foliage to reach the pulpit. Pity the poor preacher who suffers from hay fever, entering into the danger zone!

It is not only the colours I enjoy, all the lovely decorations, the various shapes and sizes and sheer variety of produce, but the smell! There is nothing like the smell of a Harvest

74

Festival, with its mixture of fruit, vegetables and flowers, and that indefinable 'church' aroma of polish, old stone, wood and books. Blended together you have a perfume that not even the most expensive bottle could contain. Rich, heady, and quite unique! As voices lift the roof, with lungs and hearts bursting with joy and praise, it is hard to keep your feet on the ground.

The great thing is that it happens every year. Oh yes, we sometimes hear that it has been a bad year for this, that or the other. Maybe a certain crop hasn't done too well, it has been too wet, too dry, too early or too late; but always there is a harvest. We have enough and to spare. We can come together and rejoice in its bounty, singing and praising God. We can sit down together and enjoy a feast of good things, with the pleasure of knowing that there is more to come, enough put by for the months ahead.

So thank God for the harvest. Let us enjoy our celebrations, fill the pews, raise the roof, and make the most of it – and then? What then? Put it behind us? Tick it off as 'done'? Start preparing for the next feast? The supermarkets are already stocked with Christmas fare, even to crackers and mincemeat.

I reckon if we are *really* grateful for the harvest, for God's goodness, for beauty, for food, for homes and families and friendship, then we should be thinking a bit more about how we could share what we have. We could dip into our pockets and give to one of the relief organisations which are trying to help the starving and the homeless. We could give some time to visiting those unable to join in our celebrations, who can't walk into church, or don't have the strength to make it to the festivities. We could give God a bit more time and attention, not just nod at him at a Harvest service, or sing his praises when he has, in a way of speaking, 'delivered the goods'. We could, and should, do all these things – and it would make a world of difference if we did. It would perhaps show that we do mean what we say and sing; that it is not just cupboard love, but genuine thanksgiving for all his provision for us, three hundred and sixty-five days a year.

After all, we eat every day. Shouldn't we also praise and share every day, as well?

What a rich harvest your goodness provides!
    Wherever you go there is plenty.
The pastures are filled with flocks;
    the hillsides are full of joy.
The fields are covered with sheep;
    the valleys are full of wheat.
Everything shouts and sings for joy. (Psalm 65.11–13 GNB)

Father, for all the joy of harvest time we thank you. For food, for fun, for beauty and celebrations we praise you. May our thanks and praise be shown not merely in words and music, but in caring and sharing every day.

31
Who's afraid?

Are you ever afraid? I don't suppose many people could put
their hand on their heart and say, 'No, never.' I know I
couldn't. I am sometimes scared stiff – particularly when the
card comes from my dentist reminding me that it is time for a
check up, and I know he is going to find something that needs
doing! It takes quite an effort to turn up on the day, and open
my mouth when he asks me. He is a kindly man, and very
gentle, and I've known him for nearly twenty years; but I'm
still scared. I tell him he is the only man I am afraid of, but
that is not true. I have quite a list of people and things and
situations that terrify me when my courage is at a low ebb.

Our fears are very personal. Many of them may seem silly
to other people, but that doesn't help us. Those silly things
grow bigger and more ferocious by the second when we are
faced with them. A spider in the bath, being shut in a lift,
walking across a room, can paralyse some people with terror.

When I was a child I was scared of going upstairs to bed. I
was convinced there was something on the stairs that would
'get me'. However much my parents reasoned with me, and
showed me there was nothing there, I was petrified. I used to
charge up the stairs into my bedroom, dive into bed and pull
the clothes over my head. Nothing ever did jump out on me,
nothing dreadful ever happened. But I was convinced it
would. I've grown out of it now, though!

I meet many people who feel vulnerable and afraid. Sadly,
in our society today we often hear of people being attacked,
and property being violated; and older people, especially
those who live alone, do have a fear of something like that
happening to them, coupled with a fear of being taken ill and
not being able to summon help. I suppose all of us are most
afraid of being alone – of the dark, the silence, the emptiness
– and not just the physical aspects, but the mental and the

77

spiritual darkness, too.

So what is the answer to fear? Or is there any answer? There are probably as many answers as there are fears. But the main thing is to do something about our fears, because left alone they grow, and can take us over; so we need to do something about them – now.

The first thing we need to do is share them. Yes, I know we feel silly talking about our fears, and we wonder what people think of us – but I can assure you, everybody knows what fear is about, and I'm sure there is somebody you could share your fears with. They may not produce an immediate answer, but just the fact of sharing will help you. Even writing down your fears helps, by bringing them out into the open, seeing them for what they are.

But you may say, 'There is no one to tell; no one I can share with.' What about God? Perhaps you had forgotten about him. He is right beside you, and his ear is always open to you. So tell him, in your own words and in your own way, what is bothering you. Tell it as it is – that is the best way.

Then it is important to face up to fears honestly. It is said that 'the Lord helps those who help themselves', and there is a lot we can do for ourselves. It is so easy to sit down and bewail our fears, to wallow in our unhappiness. When I'm feeling a bit low, that is exactly what I do. But feeling sorry for myself doesn't do me any good, in fact it makes me feel worse. Facing up to fear is painful, but not half as painful as allowing the fears to go on dominating our lives.

So, share your fears. Share them with God. Face up to them, and then forget them. Turn your back on them. Be done with them.

There is a hymn I find helpful, which has as its last verse these words:

Bringing all my burdens,
    Sorrow, sin and care.
At thy feet I lay them,
    And I leave them there.

Let's be honest – we may sing these words, we may believe

them, but do we do what they say? I wonder. We have got so used to our fears. We cling to them, we use them as excuses, as defences against launching out into life. We are like an old lady I knew who was forever bemoaning her fears and anxieties, which actually made her quite ill at times. She would not let go of them, and it was said of her, as of others like her, that she 'enjoyed ill health'.

There is one other thing about fears. Learn to laugh at them – that is the way to get rid of them. When you look fears straight in the eye and laugh, you find that they shrink, shrivel and die – that is my experience, anyway. So give it a try – laughter, the ultimate deterrent!

So then, who's afraid of what? Go on the attack, and see them run!

The Lord is my light and my salvation;
I will fear no one.
The Lord protects me from all danger;
I will never be afraid . . .
Trust in the Lord.
Have faith, do not despair.
Trust in the Lord. (Psalm 27.1,14 GNB)

Father, you know that I often feel frightened. Some of my fears are so big, I get knocked over by them. Some are such silly little things, I feel stupid speaking about them. Help me to see that nothing is too big for your power and nothing too small for your loving care. Large or small, may I hand them over to you, and leave them with you, today and always.

32
Love the Joneses

'Keeping up with the Joneses' – ah, such worldliness! We Christians don't do that sort of thing. We roll our eyes heavenwards, give our haloes a minor adjustment and say, 'Thank you, Lord, that I'm not like them. I live a simple life, as a simple, humble Christian.'

Who are the Joneses? Who are these people that the world, but definitely not us Christians, are trying to keep up with? I've been thinking about it, and I have made an interesting discovery. My own family belongs to the Jones fraternity.

We have two cars, two televisions, fitted carpets, a modern hi-fi system. We go on foreign holidays. We have a friendly bank manager, because we don't have an overdraft. We are what is termed in this part of the world, 'comfortable', and able to enjoy a considerable amount of this world's goods. When I read many articles in Christian magazines, I begin to feel more than a little guilty. For what was it that Jesus said to someone? 'Go, sell what you have . . .' But was that the whole story?

St Paul could say, 'I have learned, in whatever state I am, to be content' (RSV). He didn't say 'complacent', he didn't boast or complain, he accepted both the ups and the downs as part of God's perfect plan for him.

As I look around our neighbourhood I see plenty of Joneses. I see how poor and needy many are – poor and in need of friendship, love and understanding. I see lives which are spiritually bankrupt, with no reserve to meet the problems which affect us all – illness, worry, depression, bereavement. They are just as much in need of the love of God and of true neighbourliness as those who are on the breadline. They need someone to stand alongside them. But so often no one notices that they are in need; they are often despised, through a kind of inverted snobbery.

What matters is not what we have, or have not, but our attitude towards the things of this world. During nearly thirty years of our married life Peter and I have known hard times, lean times, and proved the power and love of God in them. We believe that as we enjoy the good things with thankful hearts, we still prove the power and love of God. We have tried to be good stewards of what we have – our time, our talents, our home and belongings, our cash and comforts. This means we can share them with others, giving them enjoyment, comfort and recreation which otherwise they might not have had.

We might have been living in an inner-city area; we could have been in desperate circumstances. We are not. We live in a pleasant part of Yorkshire, enjoy a happy life amid a congenial community. So what are we going to do about it?

We are going on doing what we have done all along – thanking God for all his goodness, seeking to share whatever he gives us, knowing that he gives us all things, the ups as well as the downs, 'richly to enjoy'.

Remember, the Joneses are people, too.

I have learnt to be satisfied with what I have. I know what it is to be in need and what it is to have more than enough. I have learnt this secret so that anywhere, at any time, I am content, whether I am full or hungry, whether I have too much or too little. I have the strength to face all conditions by the power that Christ gives me. (Philippians 4.11–13 GNB)

Teach me, Lord, to accept with joy
whatever you give me,
and with whoever you send me,
so that together we may praise
the giver.

33
A sorry tale

Everybody had worked so hard, raising money, collecting materials, emptying their wardrobes and cupboards, and now the lorry had arrived to be loaded with the results of all their efforts – food, clothing and medical supplies. Today it would leave on the first stage of its journey to bring help and hope to desperate people in need.

Everything was stacked and labelled ready to be checked on to the lorry – and the heavens opened! Emergency covers were thrown over the goods, but what was urgently needed was tarpaulins.

'No problem,' said the photographer who had come along to get some pictures for his paper. 'I know three chaps with tarpaulins, they'll lend them. Salt of the earth they are, they'll do anything for anybody.' His confidence was soon dashed.

The first man said, 'Sorry, mate, I'm busy getting the orders out.' The second replied, 'Sorry, I'm short staffed, I haven't the time.' The third responded, 'Awfully sorry, but I'm just off to play golf.'

'But it's a matter of life and death,' the photographer pleaded. 'Those supplies must get out in good condition.'

'Sorry, mate.'

'Listen, I'll mention you in the paper, give you free publicity for helping.'

'Sorry, mate.'

'It would only take you a few minutes.'

'Sorry, can't help.'

Well, those supplies did get protection. People rushed out with umbrellas, plastic macs, anything they could lay their hands on, and thankfully the rain eased off, so all was well, but no thanks to the three with the reputation of being the salt of the earth, who would do anything for anybody –

unless, of course, it slightly inconvenienced them. I don't suppose they will give it another thought. After all, they are busy making money, getting orders out, playing golf. But one day they may be in for a shock if, when they stand before God, he says to them, 'Sorry – but I don't know you.' They may need more than a tarpaulin then!

'I was hungry but you would not feed me, thirsty but you would not give me a drink; I was a stranger and you would not welcome me into your homes, naked but you would not clothe me; I was sick and in prison but you would not take care of me.' Then they will answer him, 'When, Lord, did we ever see you hungry or thirsty or a stranger or naked or sick or in prison, and would not help you?' The King will reply, 'I tell you, whenever you refused to help one of these least important ones, you refused to help me.' (Matthew 25.42–5 GNB)

Lord, thank you for reminding me of my responsibility to love and to care for those who are in need of a helping hand. As I look into their faces may I recognise that you are giving me the chance to serve you – in them, my brothers and sisters. If I am tempted to turn away, remind me of the consequences. If I am tempted to despise them, remind me of the price you paid for me.

34
Get it right!

Photography has always been a great pleasure of mine. I have no claim to being professional, but am just a very happy 'snapper', from my first little box camera, through the Instamatic, up to my present so-called 'idiot proof' one. I enjoy taking photographs, especially candid camera shots of family and friends, and local events. I must have thousands of photographs taken on holiday, at celebrations, in the parish, and recording the happenings of everyday life.

Over the years I have learned a bit about photography – the important things like making sure the lens cover is off, and putting the flash on for indoors or dull days. I like to think I have become more artistic with the camera as well, framing the scene, making sure the sun is in the right position – or rather, that I am in the right position in relation to the sun!

Recently I finished off a film and found that it would not wind back. I began to panic, thinking something had gone wrong with the camera, or the film had slipped and had been ruined. So I took it to the expert, the real photographer, who placed my camera in a black bag, sealed it up and began to unload it in the safety of the dark. I wondered why he was beaming at me, and when I asked, 'Have you discovered what went wrong?' he beamed even more. 'Oh yes, I have found the cause of the trouble. It won't cost you a penny, it's fine.' Looking at my puzzled face he added, 'You see, you had forgotten to put a film in.'

I could have kicked myself! I had never done such a stupid thing before. I suppose putting in a film had become second nature. I did it almost automatically, without thinking – except that this time I had not thought about putting it in to begin with!

I felt slightly less embarrassed when the photographer told me, 'You would be surprised how many people make the same mistake. You are not the first – or the last.' Not a great consolation, though, as I thought of all those magic moments now lost forever!

I shall now try to remind myself firmly, 'Check that you have a film in before taking photographs.' Because however carefully I position and frame the shots, whatever wonderful moments present themselves, however 'just right' the situations, unless that film is in I may as well save myself the effort of trying to record them.

Failure to attend to vital basic requirements before passing on to the seemingly more exciting things is not the only weakness of this budding amateur photographer. So many times I rush into things without thinking why, or whether I am equipped to do so. The result often turns out like my roll of film, which never was. All the effort, hard work, even the possible touches of genius, are lost, because I failed to attend to the essentials. To lose a couple of dozen photographs is unfortunate and disappointing, but far more important things can be lost through lack of foresight and plain common sense! Mind you, I don't think I shall forget to put my film in again. Being made to look a fool brought home to me the importance of taking care over details, and didn't do me any harm at all. Sometimes when our pride is hurt we get the message more quickly!

Jesus was always reminding his friends of the lessons he had tried to teach them. They needed a lot of reminding, and so he patiently and firmly went over the ground again and again. 'Remember what I told you,' he said, so that they would be able to live with confidence and be able to lead others in the right way. Time and again his friends forgot, fell flat on their faces and made a muddle of things, but once they remembered what Jesus had taught them, and got back to basics, then they were able to progress, to grow and develop, and to do the work he had called them to do.

This is the message for us, too. Get back to basics, back to observing the simple ground rules, back to checking the essentials of our faith and witness; then get on with living it out with joy and expectancy.

Tell me the old, old story, that I may take it in –
that wonderful redemption, God's remedy for sin.
Tell me the story often, for I forget so soon;
the early dew of morning has passed away at noon.

So then, my brothers, try even harder to make God's
call and his choice of you a permanent experience; if
you do so, you will never abandon your faith. In this
way you will be given the full right to enter the eternal
Kingdom of our Lord and Saviour Jesus Christ. And so
I will always remind you of these matters, even though
you already know them and are firmly grounded in the
truth you have received. (2 Peter 1.10–12 GNB)

*Lord, remind me often of your love. Remind me often of
your power. Remind me often of your call. Help me to put
you first, so that everything else will fall into the right place,
too.*
    Thank you for your constant reminders.
    Please go on reminding me – every day.
    I need it.

35
Top of the league

I am an avid reader of the sports league tables, particularly the Football League Division Two, scanning it anxiously each week to see how my favourite team is faring. I enjoy lists of all sorts. I like to imagine where I would appear in them. I do occasionally get in the religious books Bestsellers list – it does a great deal for my ego!

But the league table which caught my eye recently was one I certainly didn't figure in, or am ever likely to. It was the one listing the two hundred richest men and women in Britain. I went through it very carefully, but none of my friends appeared in it. I don't move in those circles. That is hardly surprising – even the bottom of the list was worth a cool ten million pounds.

I wonder what it feels like to be worth that much. Some of them will have grown up with it, so I suppose they take it for granted. They probably never think about – or even know about, some of them – the life of the rest of us below the top two hundred. Mind you, the article did say that the list was dominated by self-made men, and good luck to them! They have had to do it all themselves, taking huge risks, working every moment of life – and just think of the responsibility, the worry. I'm sure I couldn't take the stress of that. And probably most of them have been so busy making their pile, they have no time to spend it or enjoy it. They don't even take a day off.

Someone once said, 'Money doesn't make you happy, it just enables you to be miserable in comfort.' Well, that may be true, but I'd rather be happy any day, in comfort or not.

When I think of the really happy people I know, in the main they have little of this world's goods. They are not famous, not young or beautiful, or particularly talented. Many of them have had a rough life, having to count the pennies. And some of the happiest people I know are confined to their homes through illness or old age, or through having to look after others. They are happy, though, and it shows – and it is catching.

Happiness is a gift. You can't earn it, demand it, inherit it or manufacture it. It comes from a love of God, a love of other people, a love of life – and a thankful spirit. As the old hymn says, 'Count your blessings, name them one by one, and it will surprise you what the Lord has done.'

That is better than cash in the bank, or a place on that league table, any day.

The love of money is a source of all kinds of evil. Some have been so eager to have it that they have wandered away from the faith and have broken their hearts with many sorrows. But you, man of God, avoid all these things. Strive for righteousness, godliness, faith, love, endurance, and gentleness. (1 Timothy 6.10–11 GNB)

Lord, thank you for the cash in my pocket, the notes in my wallet, the means you have given me to pay my way. Help me to use them wisely and lovingly. May I value the responsibility, without coveting the possession, as a faithful steward of your love.

36
What did you do?

When I was a small girl, I loved to hear my grandad talk about the war. His was the Great War of 1914–18, called 'the war to end all wars'. The war took him as a young man, who had never before travelled more than a few miles, to France. It gave him many new experiences, good and bad, of army life, and eventually the joy of returning home safely to his wife and family; something, sadly that many of his young colleagues didn't have. Once home in his native West Country, he never travelled far again, but lived to a good old age in the peaceful county of Somerset.

Like all old soldiers, Grandad loved to tell his stories, show his medals and souvenirs, and proudly march to the local church on Remembrance Day, along with the small band of survivors who dwindled year by year, until he too joined the ranks of those to be remembered. We still have photos of him in uniform, his medals and the memories. I still vividly remember him and his stories. But my favourite mental picture is of him tending his immaculate garden in the village of Dunster, and his gentle West Country accent.

I remember the war – the 1939–45 one, the Second World War that began fifty years ago – it shows my age, doesn't it? I was only a small girl when it broke out, a teenager when it ended. I have my memories of wartime, of evacuees, food parcels, American G Is who gave me gum and Hershey Bars – yes, I was one of those who shouted, 'Got any gum, chum?'. Memories of gas masks, air raid shelters, ration books, newsreels, and a thousand and one other things. I have no medals, though – but I do have a letter of thanks from Mrs Churchill for collecting 'Aid to Russia', and a certificate saying I had 'attained the rank of Field Marshal in the Book Collection'. I wonder what became of my collection of army badges. Maybe I swapped them for something else – I can't remember.

Sharing memories and stories of earlier days is an important part of life. Remembering the past helps us to see life in perspective, and to realise, even faintly, that what happened yesterday affects our today, and tomorrow. We do well to listen to, and give thanks for, those who like my grandad, responded to the call of 'King and Country': those G Is, only boys then, who came over to help us in the war, and the friends who sent us food parcels when we needed them. We made lifelong friends during the war, and are still corresponding with Americans three generations on. We are one family, we belong together, and that is great.

We are all part of one family, whoever we are. None of us is self-sufficient. We need one another, even though we may not recognise, or want to recognise, that fact. I can look back and see that I lived through a very important part of the history of the world. It didn't seem like it at the time; only now is it being revealed. The sobering thought is, I am still living through momentous times now. All of us are. We are part of history in the making, and we are making memories for others to enjoy – or endure.

What we are doing and saying now will affect those who come after us, their quality of life, their future. Perhaps we are beginning to get the message, and that is why we have suddenly become aware of our environment, and are trying to do something before it is too late. We are realising that 'green is beautiful', and looking after the earth's resources, instead of just taking and squandering them without thinking.

Well, 'While there's life there's hope' – and while we have life, let us use it wisely, to give our children and grandchildren a legacy for the future. I don't mean a few pounds in the Building Society, or a timeshare in a Spanish villa, but something far more important: memories of love and care and fun and faith.

Today is an opportunity we all have. Let's celebrate the gift of life by putting something good into it. Let's give with love to God who gave us our life; with love to those who share our life with us today; and with love to those who will have to get on with the job of making sense of it all in the future.

Think of the past, of the time long ago;
    ask your fathers to tell you what happened,
    ask the old men to tell of the past.
(Deuteronomy 32.7 GNB)

Father,
Help me to remember and learn from the past,
to live lovingly and responsibly today,
so that those who come after
may look back with thanksgiving,
and praise your name.

37
This means you!

I do quite a lot of travelling in my job – not usually to exotic places, mainly within twenty miles radius of my home, with occasional forays further afield. I know this patch of North Yorkshire like the back of my hand. I sometimes think I could say 'giddy-up' to the car, and it would go on its own.

But the other day I was driving along a familiar route, one where I could tell you every bump, twist and turn in the road, when I saw a notice: 'Road closed ahead'.

'No it isn't,' I said to myself, without even reducing speed. 'I know it isn't.' I had done the journey only a couple of days before.

A mile further on was another, larger notice: 'Road closed ahead'. I dropped my speed momentarily, then thought, 'Well, it may be to strangers, but not to *me*.'

About half a mile from my destination an even bigger sign with an arrow proclaimed: 'Road closed ahead. Diversion.'

I began to think that maybe there was something happening ahead. I slowed down and considered the situation. My car is only a little one; it could get round any obstruction, I decided. I was almost at the end of my journey, I just had to go under the old railway bridge and . . . It wasn't there any more! They had taken it down in the night, and I wouldn't even have got through on my push bike.

I was a bit cross as I turned the car round and went back, following the diversion sign, then I laughed to myself: 'It serves you right – you won't be told.' And I thought, isn't that just like life? We think we know all there is to know, we have done the same thing so often, and then God says, 'Stop!' But: 'No, you can't mean me; you're talking to someone else. And anyway, even if there is trouble ahead I can squeeze through. I'll be all right' . . . until we come round a bend in life and find that God was right after all. It's no use trying that way, it's a dead end – there is no other way through.

The great thing is, though, that if only we'll realise we are running into danger, going into a dead end; if only we'll shelve our pride and not press on pig-headedly, but turn round; we'll see that there *is* another way, a better way, the way he provides for us – and it leads to life.

Jesus was once asked about the way to heaven and how to get there. He said, 'I am the way, the truth and the life . . . *follow me.*' I reckon if we do that, we won't go far wrong.

The Lord is my shepherd, I shall not want;
    he makes me lie down in green pastures.
He leads me beside still waters:
    he restores my soul.
He leads me in paths of righteousness
    for his name's sake.
Even though I walk through the valley of
      the shadow of death,
  I fear no evil;
for thou art with me;
    thy rod and thy staff,
      they comfort me. (Psalm 23.1–4 RSV)

Lord, show me your way,
and give me the sense to follow it.
– and when I stray from it
    give me the grace to admit my failure
    and start again.

38
This is the day

I was flicking through a magazine, when my eye was caught by the headline: 'Today is everything'. The article described the importance of living each day as it comes, and it ended by saying, 'There are no yesterdays except in history, there are no tomorrows except in hope. Yesterday is a cancelled cheque, tomorrow a promissory note, but today is ready cash.'

I thought of this a few days later when I met a radiant newly-wed, with stars in her eyes. She was well into her forties, and told me she had just got married to a widower, over twenty years her senior. 'I know there's a great age difference,' she said, 'and maybe we won't have all that long together, but we are living and enjoying every day as it comes. Every day is a beautiful gift, and we are making the most of living.'

I hope those two people will have many happy years together. They have got the right attitude, haven't they? Today is for living.

Each morning when I wake up, whatever the weather, whatever I knows lies ahead, I say very firmly, 'This is the day the Lord has made. I will rejoice and be glad in it.' That is not original thinking, it is a straight quote from Psalm 118 – but I have found over many years that it has really helped me, not only to get through each day, but to find in each day joy and satisfaction.

Starting the day with those words helps me to 'get out of bed on the right side' – with a note of cheerfulness, thankfulness and optimism. It is more than just positive thinking. I am trying to say thank you to God for the ready cash of time he places in my hands each day. Seconds, minutes, hours – opportunities not to be selfishly hoarded or carelessly squandered, but to be used and delighted in. It is ready cash – it

94

can't be carried forward. Like Cinderella's coach, it vanishes at midnight.

Let us live today so that tomorrow there will be no regrets and no debts, just 'Lived in full' written on our page of history.

I will always thank the Lord;
    I will never stop praising him.
I will praise him for what he has done. (Psalm 34.1–2 GNB)

Thank you, Father, for this day,
thank you for the beauty of creation,
for the joy of living,
for love to share,
and for your love so freely given.
Thank you, Father.

39
Be ready

The gentle reminders begin to gather speed and volume as the time approaches. With only one month to go, it is impossible to ignore them. All our senses are assailed. Words, music, shop window displays, lights, draw our attention to the coming event, and the need to be ready. 'Post early for Christmas.' – 'Order your Christmas turkey now.' – 'Buy now to avoid disappointment.' – and so we all join in the mad scramble to make ready. We have sleepless nights wondering how we are going to fit everything in before the great day; because it doesn't bear thinking about not to be one hundred per cent ready and waiting, with everything 'done and dusted', so that we can celebrate with happiness, relief and a clear conscience.

As we make our last frantic efforts in the annual run up to Christmas, we have no excuse for not knowing that the day is fast approaching. How silly we would look if we said, 'But no one told me.'; 'I never thought it would happen so soon.'

Yet the weeks of Advent carry another important message, which we tend to ignore; a message, not of a past event to be celebrated, but of *the* most momentous event to come – the end of the world and of all things. That puts a damper on the proceedings, doesn't it? We begin to wriggle, we change the subject, and rush off to buy yet another bauble for the Christmas tree, and remember that Auntie Jane asked us to call, and . . . and . . . anything rather than listen to the message, the relentless reminder to 'be ready'. Ready, not to celebrate the first coming of Jesus as a baby, born in a stable at Bethlehem, but the second coming of Christ in glory, 'to judge the living and the dead'.

The great themes of Advent are the resurrection of the dead, the final judgement, and the creation of the new heaven and the new earth. Not very Christmassy themes, as someone reminded me a few years ago when on Advent Sunday, the fourth Sunday before Christmas, I preached on Christ's second coming. She gave me a very severe look and said, 'That's enough to put anyone off their Christmas dinner.' To which I replied, 'And how do you know you are going to get one?'

Jesus the baby, Jesus small and defenceless, Jesus in humble surroundings; that is all right. He is no threat. He makes a nice centre-piece to our celebrations, our chance to forget the gloom of winter and 'eat, drink and be merry'. As with any baby at such times, we hope he will sleep through the adult goings-on. And anyway, a baby would not know what was happening, even if the party was supposed to be in his honour – rather like some christening parties, a pleasant excuse for a party and a cake.

But Jesus Christ coming in power to judge – well, that is not so attractive. In fact it is rather frightening; we prefer to forget that part of the Christian story. Yet it too is good news, something to make us glad – otherwise what is there to look forward to in the future? I believe that the Jesus I have come to know and love in this life already, will come again. I believe that he will be seen face to face; that his coming will signal the end of history, and that 'he shall reign for ever and ever'. I believe, too, that I will be there to take part in it, to enjoy the new heaven and the new earth. A glorious eternity in his presence – that is enough for me.

I have already started out on the new life. I am living it now, very imperfectly, and in a very limited fashion – limited by the restrictions of this present existence. But I look forward to the time when all those imperfections and limitations will be done with; because Jesus promises that it will be so for all those who trust him – and I do.

So the weeks of Advent are for looking forward, beyond the celebration of Christmas, beyond this life; and I need reminding that I have to be ready, to be working, watching, sharing the news with others. What have I got to look forward to? Everything! What abou you?

People will faint from fear as they wait for what is coming over the whole earth, for the powers in space will be driven from their courses. Then the Son of Man will appear, coming in a cloud with great power and glory. When these things begin to happen, stand up and raise your heads, because your salvation is near. (Luke 21.26–8 GNB)

Lord Jesus Christ,
As we delight to prepare to celebrate your first coming as a
baby at Bethlehem, may we delight to prepare for your
second coming with even more eagerness and expectation.
Keep us alert, watchful and working, so that when your
new day dawns, we may not be left out of the eternal
celebrations. In your name we pray.

40
Who is responsible?

'If this is God's world, it's about time he did something about it. Just look at the mess it's in.'

I hear that said often, and maybe it is understandable, considering the things that happen in the world. It must be someone's responsibility to look after things here on earth.

Jesus talked a lot about responsibility. Listen to his words, recorded in Matthew's Gospel:

> Who then is the faithful and wise servant, whom his master has set over his household, to give them their food at the proper time? Blessed is that servant whom his master when he comes will find so doing. Truly, I say to you, he will set him over all his possessions. But if that wicked servant says to himself, 'My master is delayed,' and begins to beat his fellow servants, and eats and drinks with the drunken, the master of that servant will come on a day when he does not expect him and at an hour he does not know, and will punish him, and put him with the hypocrites; there men will weep and gnash their teeth. (Matthew 24.45–51 RSV)

This is God's world. He has made it, it belongs to him, so he is in charge. But he has put people in the world to take care of it. Call them stewards, servants, friends – the title doesn't really matter. What does matter is that they get on with the job, caring for the world, the natural resources, the animal kingdom, and for all the people who live here, the family of man that keeps growing. Everybody must be catered for, and special attention must be given to those who are in particular need: the starving, the homeless, the handicapped and disabled, those who have no one to stand up for them. There is a lot that needs to be done.

So who are these stewards, or servants, or friends, or

whatever you like to call them? They don't seem to be very effective, do they? It makes me wonder whether they realise what a responsibility they have. They seem to be asleep on the job, or turning a blind eye to it. Maybe some of them are busy lining their own pockets, the selfish lot! It will serve them right if when God calls them to account they come a cropper.

But the frightening thing is, that one of the people entrusted with the job of caring is me . . . and you, as well; all of us, in fact. So what would you do if you were called to account? What would I do?

I think I would plead for more time, for another chance. I'd say I hadn't realised that time was so short; I hadn't really seen what needed doing; and I didn't think I would be called to account so soon.

But then, it could be, I would be reminded of what I had read so many times in the Bible about *my* responsibility – and then I would not have a leg to stand on, would I? Maybe you have got a better excuse.

Perhaps, though, it would be better for us all to be honest, and admit we've failed, and asked for another chance, another day.

O Lord, forgive us for the way we have failed you,
for all the excuses we make.
Thank you that today is an opportunity from you to do better.
Help us to take it.

41
Love one another

There was a case reported in the newspapers of a man who
was convicted of stealing, not cash or expensive goods but
Christmas cards which he hung round his room to prove to
himself that he had friends. I felt it was not the man who
should have been convicted, but all of us who fail to recognise
the cry for help of people like him – and there are many who
are desperate for friendship yet fail to communicate their
need because of their shyness and others' indifference.

It makes me think of a young man in our parish who is
dreadfully shy, and it has taken us a long time to convince
him that he really matters, that we do want him. Or the girl
who is so aggressive and puts everyone's back up, yet again is
crying out for friendship. It is difficult to get through to
either of them, and I know I am often tempted to write them
off. And yet these are the people most in need of real friends.
It is easy to get along with people who are good company,
who think like I do, and enjoy the same things. With other
people, I need to make that extra effort to spend time with
them and draw them into the circle. If we are to make such a
friendship, we must be prepared for hard work.

Friendship is a delicate plant. Often people who have at
some time been hurt and rejected are very wary of making
new relationships. And then there are the friends who let us
down, abuse our confidence, or take us for granted. Friendship can also be a dangerous business. It means you are
vulnerable, you have to open up your inner self, and that can
be painful.

There are times when I am tempted to say, 'That finishes
it.' But then I remember the way Jesus made friends, and
who he made friends with – and how did they repay him?
One, Judas, betrayed him, another claimed he never even
knew him, several slept through the time when Jesus most

needed their support, and others just ran off. For Jesus, this must have been as much a part of his suffering as the physical pain of the cross – and yet he was still willing to make friends right to the end. As his followers, can we do less?

But perhaps I have painted a gloomy picture. There is the other side to friendship. I think of the old lady who says, 'I know you are busy, luv, so I've made you a cake,' or the man next door who is willing to get out of bed to start my car, even though he has just come off night shift. I think of the friends who will listen to me without saying 'I told you so', or 'If I were you . . .', and the friends who are brave enough to tell me where I am going wrong, *and* what I must do about it.

I thank God for my friends, those I have had for many years, and the ones I have made recently; those who support me with their love and prayers, and with the little acts of kindness and affection which they do because I am their friend.

It has been said that the real friend is the one who knows you as you really are, and loves you just the same – and because I am so grateful for those who stick to me through thick and thin, I am able to go on holding out the hand of friendship to others, even when occasionally it gets bitten. For if we are Christians, then we are called to be friends, real friends, even to the point of death. On the night before he died, Jesus said this about friendship:

My commandment is this: love one another just as I love you. The greatest love a person can have for his friends is to give his life for them. And you are my friends if you do what I command you . . . love one another. (John 15.12–14, 17 GNB)

Lord Jesus Christ,
If you could love me enough
to die for me,
you must think I'm worth it.

If you could love others enough
to die for them,
you must think they are worth it too.
May the measure of your love
be reflected in mine,
in loving obedience
to your command.

42
All switched on

Christmas seems to come earlier every year – the preparations, I mean. I know it is sensible to prepare well in advance;
but snapping up Christmas cards and gifts in the January
sales – well, it must rob Christmas of some of its excitement.
So I don't start that much in advance, but I do try to make my
cakes a couple of months beforehand, to let them mature;
and of course there are the overseas letters and parcels to get
into the post. But I must confess to being fairly last-minute
with most of the other preparations.

Christmas really dawns on me when I see the 'lights'
switched on in Selby. For a small town our lights are
absolutely marvellous. So much time and trouble and effort
goes in each year to make the display even better than the
year before, and with the Christmas tree in the town centre
beside the ancient Abbey, it looks just like one of those old
fashioned Christmas card scenes. So when the lights are
switched on, I too feel 'switched on'; for me, Christmas has
begun, and I can see in the faces and feel in the attitudes of
others that it affects them in the same way.

When I look at those twinkling lights I always think of the
words of Jesus when he said, 'I am the light of the world.' He
came to dispel the darkness, and it certainly was a dark world
into which he was born. It was tough living in those days.
Life was cheap and short; cruelty, oppression and ignorance
seemed to have the upper hand. A dark period of history
indeed.

Yet has much changed after two thousand years? In spite
of all our advances, so that we can watch events across the
world as they actually happen, and with all the wonders of
technology which make life so much easier for many of us,
people are still much the same as they always were. We have
only to pick up a newspaper, or switch on the radio or

television, to realise how many dark places there are in the world; all the dark deeds being done, the blackness of hate and despair that threatens to engulf us all.

As I look into my own heart and life there are plenty of dark corners. I have my black spots, too. But there is always light, because Jesus has come. St John described his coming in the words: 'The light shines in darkness and the darkness has never put it out.' That is gloriously true; right from the time of his coming into the world on that first Christmas, the light has never been put out. It has burned low at times, as many people have had a go at trying to snuff Jesus out, but his light goes on shining. In the darkness of human experience, it is the divine spark which is present in every man and woman.

I live in the country, a few miles out of town, so it is pretty dark in winter driving home at night, but at Christmas time the lights shine from every window – isolated cottages, farmhouses, village pubs. Some folk put lights in the trees in their gardens, and as I drive past, on a starlit night – well, it is a little bit of heaven on earth.

I suppose that is what Christmas is, a bit of heaven right here on earth! But it is easy to get sentimental and forget what else Jesus said about the light – which was that we are to be lights as well. We have all got to do our part in bringing light into the dark places, to be shining examples in our homes, at work and in our community.

There is a children's hymn that goes like this:

Jesus bids us shine with a pure, clear light
Like a little candle burning in the night.
In this world of darkness, so we must shine,
You in your small corner, and I in mine.

Kid's stuff, you might say, but I tell you it isn't. It's hard work being a light, and especially being a pure, clear light. When at the office party you are asked to do something you know you shouldn't, with 'Come on, don't be a spoil sport – it's Christmas'; when all the hassle has got you down and you snap back with an unkind or sharp reply; or when, seeing others splash their money around, you feel envious and angry; as the temptations crowd in, it is easy to give in, and to be swept along with the darkness. Sometimes even the sheer pace of Christmas plunges us into the blackness of despair, into that feeling of being unable to cope with it all.

Well, Jesus bids you shine! He wants you to shine, and – this is the joy of it – he enables you to shine; because he provides the power and the energy. All we have to do is come close to him and catch on to his light. As I look at the Christmas lights, as I look at Jesus, I am opening myself up to the light; I am coming out of the darkness and the shadows into his pure, clear light. The flame of his love reaches out to me, so that I can receive his light and so light the way for someone else.

The message of Christmas is: 'The light has come – pass it on!' The message is to you and to me. Yes, 'you in your small corner, and I in mine.' Let's shine, shall we – for him!

In the beginning was the Word, and the Word was with God, and the Word was God. He was in the beginning with God; all things were made through him, and without him was not anything made that was made. In him was life, and the life was the light of men. The light shines in the darkness, and the darkness has not overcome it. (John 1.1–5 RSV)

Jesus, light of the world, shine in my darkness.
Jesus, light of the world, kindle a flame in my heart.
Jesus, light of the world, help me to shine for you.

43
All things new

For years now, my friends have been trying to persuade me to go over to Filofax, that rolling diary and container of everything I need to know about every day. I have resisted, and will go on resisting, for one good reason – I enjoy having a new diary for each year! There is something very special and meaningful for me about opening a brand new diary with its bright, uncrumpled pages. I don't want one year to merge into another without a special marker. I want to close the pages of my tattered old diary and open a brand new one on January 1st.

All right, I know there is nothing magical about a diary, or a date, but I still find it exciting to start a new year with a clean sheet – or lots of clean sheets. At the end of each December I look back on my year, and my crumpled, tattered diary helps me to do so. I think about all the people I have met, my appointments, meetings, the situations in which I found myself. The scribbled comments and the notes in my own shorthand, remind me of the year that has gone. I transfer the things I need to carry over into my new diary, and then I commend the old year to the Lord, praying for forgiveness for the wrongs I have done, thanking him for the joys I have had, and asking for his grace and help in the 'transfers'. I keep all my old diaries in a neat orderly row on the top shelf of my office. They form a sort of record of my life, of things done with, accounted for, given to God.

As I write my name and address on the front page of my new diary, I offer that to God as well – the year ahead, with all those blank pages, all that space. A new start!

I usually try and stay up to see the new year in, for it is a marker in my life, as it is in yours. The calendar changes, and somehow there is always that surge of hope, that it really will be 'a good New Year'. Sometimes we have held a 'watch-

night' service at St James'. They used to be very popular, but
sadly many people are afraid to go out late at night now. This
is a pity, because to end the year in God's house, with others
of his family, and to begin anew with them in that place, has a
special sort of feel about it. Yet whether we begin in church,
with a family gathering, with friends, or by ourselves, we are
still in God's presence, and are part of his family, on earth
and in heaven.

It is good to stand still, to look back and to look forward, to
take a deep breath before rushing on, allowing the Lord to
steady us and set us straight; and then to start out with
confidence and hope – not in ourselves, but in him, the one
who makes all things new – people included.

'A happy New Year' – Yes, we all look forward hopefully,
we all want to be happy; but maybe I would rather say 'a
joyful New Year'. Many years ago now I heard someone
describe the difference between happiness and joy: 'Happiness depends on happenings, joy depends on Jesus.' No
doubt during this coming year there will be lots of happenings in our lives; some will make us happy, others unhappy,
that is the way it goes. Yet I know, and I have proved in my
life, that Jesus brings joy – yes, in good times and bad,
because he is there, he shares in our life, and he doesn't let go.

A new year, a new diary, new hopes. May it always be for
us a joy-full new year, and may the joy of the Lord be always
with us, every day.

Remember not the former things,
    nor consider the things of old.
Behold, I am doing a new thing;
    now it springs forth, do you not perceive it?
(Isaiah 43.18–19 RSV)

Lord,
Thank you that you have dealt with the past;
it is over and done.
Thank you for all that lies ahead,
for you are there already.

44
Personal delivery

One of the highlights of my year is the school nativity play, always held the day before the children break up for the Christmas holidays. By the time it takes place, after all the build-up, and with the prospect of the party in the afternoon, the air is electric. The children are so excited that, like tightly-wound springs, they are likely to snap and fly off in all directions. So although the nativity play is always the same story – well, it has to be, hasn't it? – and the same costumes are brought out of store, and the props arranged in the same way, each 'production' has its own unique touch, an incident that sets it apart in the memory for years to come.

Last year's was no exception; the play was moving along at a good pace, and the young Mary had coped beautifully with the visitation of the angel, the birth and the shepherds' visit – in fact she hadn't taken all that much interest in the shepherds, but gave them rather a disdainful look, as if to say, 'Don't go messing up my stable, sit down and be quiet – and take that lamb away from my baby!'

Then came the visit of the wise men. As usual they trod on each other's cloaks and made a less than dignified entrance. But young Mary sat there wide-eyed, obviously delighted to see them – or rather, to see what they had brought. They presented their gold, frankincense and myrrh, three carefully gift-wrapped parcels, each one of a different shape, decorated with tinsel. Mary beamed her thanks and then, ignoring the givers, Joseph, the baby, the angels and the congregation, sat and unwrapped the gifts – an unscripted 'commercial break'. Eventually, with the aid of some stage whispers, she was persuaded to put the parcels down and get on with the play; but she hadn't the same interest in it. All she was interested in was discovering what was in the parcels. It was the most exciting bit for her – and great fun for us.

That six-year-old Mary gave me a fresh insight into the Gospel account of the visit of the Magi. I must have read the story hundreds of times, seen it portrayed in so many different ways, from school and church nativity plays to film versions and the famous York Mystery Plays; but I had missed out on something very special – the sheer excitement and wonder, for an ordinary country girl, of the visit of those great men with their strange gifts.

Perhaps the gold was used to finance the journey to Egypt, and to provide for the family while they were refugees. But what of the frankincense and myrrh – those symbols of the great high priest who would be sacrificed for love's sake? Whatever happened to them? Mary must often have turned them over in her mind, and as the years went by would have experienced the reality of their prophetic significance.

Were there three wise men, or more? Were they kings, or scholars, or what? How long did their journey take? While for the benefit of nativity plays and carol services we combine their visit with that of the shepherds, it would seem that they arrived much later. The Bible account refers to 'the child' rather than a baby, and as Herod ordered the massacre of all the boys under the age of two, it could have been any time up to two years after the birth.

In the Church's year, January 6th is set apart as 'the Epiphany' – the 'showing' of Jesus to the Gentiles, the world beyond the Jewish nation. Foreigners, outsiders, were prepared to follow the star to find the King. They were prepared to offer their gifts to a child who looked anything but a king, in anything but royal surroundings. They made one mistake – an almost disastrous one, but for God's intervention – when they relied on their own ideas rather than on the guiding light; but they were soon on course again, and came to discover the object of their journey.

Some people find the journey to faith simple and direct, rather like the shepherds who only had to nip down the hill. Many others have to go by a long and arduous route, sometimes with costly and fruitless detours. But what matters is the arrival point, and not the journey. Maybe you are still travelling on that journey, not really knowing where you are going, but carrying your gifts with you. When you do arrive, you will know; and you will feel free to offer your personal gifts. But when? Where? Take heart! We all make a different journey, because we all start from different points. We are all hindered by our own ideas, our expectations, our conditioning and cultures. But if we honestly look for God's guidance we will find it. And if we keep our eyes fixed on our goal, then sure enough he will lead us to himself, and will receive our gifts from us with joy and delight. And we will worship face to face him who is our King, our Priest and our Life.

Doesn't that make the journey, however long it takes, however much it costs us, worth while?

When they saw the star, they rejoiced exceedingly with great joy; and going into the house they saw the child with Mary his mother, and they fell down and worshipped him. Then, opening their treasures, they offered him gifts, gold and frankincense and myrrh. (Matthew 2.10–11 RSV)

Lord, keep my eyes fixed on the way that leads to you. Give me the courage, the wisdom and the humility to rely on your guidance rather than on my own ideas. Thank you for the gifts you have given me. I offer them to you to be used in your service and for your glory.

45
Shedding some light

From the moment we are born until we die we are affected by other people, for good or ill. We don't always recognise this until perhaps years later when something happens in our life which 'rings a bell'. Then we realise that the way we have reacted has been largely coloured by earlier experiences which until then had lain dormant, but still very much alive, in our memory bank.

I suppose the biggest influences in life are those of childhood – parents, family, teachers, school friends, those who helped us in our growing up process. Sadly, of course, some people can be terrible influences, and leave a mark which is hard to remove. Some people are scarred for life, mentally and emotionally as well as physically, because of something that happened to them. Today we are becoming all too aware of child abuse and its consequences and of other stresses and strains placed upon children, depriving them of innocence and childhood.

But think of the good influences, the people you can look back on and say, 'They were good to me.' – 'She was marvellous.' – 'He was a real pal.' You know that life would have been poorer without them – and now you can say, 'Thank God they were there.'

The church school I went to until I was eleven was a happy school; it was small and, with the church, was the centre of the community where 'everybody knew everybody else'. Friendships made then have lasted, and the memories are good ones, which have influenced my life and attitudes.

So going into school each week as I do now is almost a continuation of those happy days, for Wistow school is not a big school, not by most standards anyway. There are around ninety children aged four plus to eleven, with a first class staff and helpers, and supported by the 'Friends of Wistow

School', mostly parents and ex-pupils. On Fridays the vicar and I go there to take assembly, and as soon as the children see us they want to tell us everything at once, chatting about what they have been doing, showing us anything they have new, and sharing their secrets.

One Friday in January I got there early to rig up my visual aids before they came in. I was going to talk about the story Jesus told of the lamp under the bucket, and so I had got my bedside lamp hidden under the Christmas tree tub. They were very curious to find out what was under there, and made all sorts of suggestions, but of course as soon as I told the story they realised what it was.

I must confess I enjoy surprising them; I reckon they remember the story better that way. They surprise me too, especially with the questions they ask – no messing about, no hedging round things, out it comes. I often get put on the spot.

That January morning a little girl stayed behind when the others went rushing off, and looking up at me very solemnly asked, 'Mrs Cundiff, how is it you know so much about Jesus?'

Looking at her was like looking into a mirror, nearly fifty years ago. I saw myself in her. She even looks like I did at her age, a sturdy, fair-haired child who furrows her brows when she talks. I suddenly had a picture of my old school – there were no carpets or bright furniture then, it was plain wooden floors and desks, and no central heating. But I could hear myself saying those same words to our local vicar who used to come in to take our assemblies. I was fascinated by someone who seemed to be on such close terms with God, because he always talked about him in a very informed and personal way, and who showed in his face the reality of God and his love.

So here I was with the tables turned. Now someone was puting me in the hot seat. Children's questions can be pretty devastating. I would like to think I gave her a memorable answer, but I doubt it. I tried to explain that I had been finding out about Jesus ever since I was her age, and so had a good few years experience.

Her question has stayed with me, though. I have thought about it quite a lot since, and I have been reminded how much I owe to the faithful, godly man who not only told me about Jesus, but showed me him too. My mum and dad, teachers, and friends, have all been links in the chain over the last fifty-odd years, and I'm still finding out, still learning.

You could say it is a very different world today from the one when I was a child. Today's children are far more sophisticated. Christian teaching and Christian values are not the norm as they were in my schooldays. Yet goodness and truth surely never go out of fashion, however much passing trends and fads may try to say otherwise.

So week by week, when I go to school, I shall hope and pray that the children won't just hear about Jesus, but that they may get a glimpse of him. I'll try not to stand in the way.

No one lights a lamp and puts it under a bowl; instead he puts it on the lampstand, where it gives light for everyone in the house. In the same way, your light must shine before people, so that they will see the good things you do and praise your Father in heaven. (Matthew 5.15–16 GNB)

Lord,
Thank you for those who have lit up my life
with goodness, truth and love.
Help me to show and share
the light of your love
with those I meet today.

46
Union man

Don is a member of our deanery synod. We were having a
problem trying to fix a date for our next meeting; as of course
there are only seven evenings in a week, it is difficult to find a
time to suit everybody. Don said Thursday was out – he had a
meeting most Thursdays which couldn't be altered.

Eventually, when we had found a date which suited everybody, I happened to say to Don, 'Do you have your house
group on Thursdays?'

Don looked surprised. 'Oh, no. It's nothing to do with the
church. I'm on my Union branch committee. I'm a shop
steward.'

It was quite a shock. He didn't look the militant type to
me, and yet the industry he works in is quite renowned for its
union action.

'What made you take that on?' I asked, and he began to
explain to me how he got involved.

'It's no use grumbling if you're not prepared to do something,' he said. 'Once I got on the committee I realised how
important it was for me to be there as a Christian – a bit of
"leaven in the lump", I hope.'

Don makes his union work a high priority. It can't be easy,
for he has to take quite a bit of criticism. He told me how sad
he feels when others see his union work as not being anything
to do with his faith: 'You pray for the Sunday school teachers'
meeting, but how about praying for me at my union meeting?' I took the point, and I do try to remember him and his
colleagues regularly in my prayers.

We often label activities 'Christian' or 'non-Christian', but
as Don reminded me, it is the people in the organisation, not
what the organisation is called, which makes it either Christian or non-Christian. He sees it as just as much a commit-
ment to Christ to be at his union meeting as to be on the

parochial church council or the deanery synod.

Of course it is easier to fill our time with meetings connected with our church, to be in the company of Christian friends, to talk religious language, to stay in our safe and secure parochial organisations. Yet Jesus told us to 'Go into all the world with the good news.' We often interpret that as 'Make your world within the fellowship at church.'

Christians are needed at every level of decision-making: on the local council, trade union branch, social club, parent/ teachers association, police liaison committee, village hall, pensioners' club, and so on. You may be the only Christian voice on that group, but you are a voice. As a member of the community you are entitled to a voice, and you must earn the respect of others if that voice is to be heard.

We need the Dons to be the voices, to be the witnesses. They need our support, our interest and our prayers so that they do not feel alone, so that they know they have the backing not just of card-carrying colleagues but of praying friends.

Are you a union man or woman? If so, as a member shouldn't you be prepared to vote with more than your feet?

Jesus asked, 'What shall I compare the Kingdom of God with? It is like this. A woman takes some yeast and mixes it with forty litres of flour until the whole batch of dough rises.' (Luke 13.20–21 GNB)

Thank you, Father, for those who serve their fellow men and women in industry and commerce, who take responsibility in their trade unions, committees and professional bodies. Grant them wisdom, insight and courage in their service, and strength of body, mind and spirit to enable them to fulfil their calling.

47
Forecast for today

Whenever I am asked to speak at a meeting, to 'preach away', or do a radio series, I always look at the date and wonder, 'What will the weather be like then?' I have been caught out many times, making arrangements in May for the following March, and come March I have become a worried weather watcher as the appointment loomed ever nearer.

So when I was asked to do 'Pause for Thought' for thirteen weeks from January to March, my heart sank. Not because of the programme – I love it – but January through to March! I had visions of plodding through six feet of snow – and being only five foot two, that could present difficulties! And what about fog, ice, and the dark mornings? To add to my problems, one of the two bridges from Selby into York was due to be closed, so the traffic would be doubly heavy; it is bad at the best of times. And I always get a cold and lose my voice some time during the winter, particularly after Christmas.

So I thought about it, prayed about it, and said – 'I'll do it!'
. . . And I did it, and we had no snow, ice or fog, at least not on Thursday mornings, when I drove into York to do my spot. The bridge closure was put off until April, and in spite of the traffic I always made it to the studio in time. I did get a cold, but I didn't lose my voice – not that you would notice, anyway. So my fears evaporated before my very eyes, and any little problems – well, like the bridges, I crossed them when I came to them.

I would like to think I have learned something by this. After all, I am always telling others to trust the Lord, and sometimes I worry myself sick over the silliest little things. But I am not unique in that. I have talked to some of the most important, saintly and talented people, and found that they too get butterflies, and cold feet, and have sleepless nights

117

from time to time, just worrying over what *might* happen.

Let's face it, we all encounter problems and difficulties in our lives, but worrying about them won't make a scrap of difference; all it will do is magnify them, and destroy our peace of mind today.

There is some very good advice in the book of Proverbs: 'Trust in the Lord with all your heart. Never rely on what you think you know. Remember the Lord in everything you do, and he will show you the right way.' (Proverbs 3.5 GNB)

It is easy to quote that, but not always quite so easy to do it; and sometimes I have my off-days – don't we all! But then I remember how God has got me through my life this far, and not just through January to March, and so I know I can trust him; it's a proven fact.

I travel a lot in my car, and when I am driving along I often sing – unless I have passengers; they might not appreciate the music! One particular favourite song of mine is 'One more step along the world I go':

> As I travel through the bad and good
> Keep me travelling the way I should –
> Where I see no way to go
> You'll be telling me the way, I know.
> And it's from the old I travel to the new,
> Keep me travelling along with you.

Of course, I try to use my common sense, and my road sense too. I carry a road map, I use my eyes, I observe signs and signals; but I know that, whatever happens, nothing will ever separate me from the Lord, not life or death; and he will get me safely to the end of my journey this day, and every day of my earthly travels.

> God knows every step I take . . .
> I follow faithfully the way he chooses,
>   and never wander to either side.
> I always do what God commands;
>   I follow his will, not my own desires. (Job 23.10–12 GNB)

Thank you, Lord, for all your guidance and your direction in my life, for getting me safely through my life this far. Help me to trust you, and to travel joyfully with you, today and every day.

48
With a little help from my friends

I love radio stations. I love the noise, the action, the people. I love the cup of coffee that is pressed into my hand as soon as I go through the door. I love having colleagues around me whom I can depend on to make sure all the technical work is done. I love the security that gives me. And of course, if anything goes wrong, then there is always someone else to blame!

Most of my broadcasting is done from such studios; but every few months I have my week of early morning broadcasting 'Just a Thought' from the Goole studio, which is a small, unmanned satellite of BBC Radio Humberside. It is a tiny, box-like place, beside the public library. I collect the key from the police station across the road, open up, switch on, sort everything out, and connect up with the main studio in Hull. It is a strange feeling, particularly on dark, cold, miserable mornings, to be sitting there all alone. It feels as though I am the only person awake in the world. I could be anywhere, for the studio has no identity of its own; it is just a box.

Being in that studio, though, does a great deal for my ego. I am in charge of it. I do everything myself; I put myself 'on air', speak to the eager waiting thousands – well, to whoever happens to be listening at that hour – and I feel very proud of myself. The sense of power is quite overwhelming.

That feeling soon goes, though, as I begin to think about what is really happening. I am just part of a team of unseen and mainly unheard people who enable my voice to go out over the radio. The technological miracles which are placed at my disposal, the planning of the station staff, the engineers at the other end in Hull, the presenter of the Breakfast Show who brings me in at just the right moment – all combine together to enable me to share my 'Just a Thought'. I may be physically alone, I may even feel alone; but I am not. I am part of an organisation geared to supporting and enabling that programme, and my slot in it, to be effective.

We all have times of feeling absolutely alone, particularly if we are going through a dark patch, when the world seems cold and unfeeling towards us. Equally we have our moments of glorious self-sufficiency, when we think we can manage very well on our own, we don't need anyone else, thank you very much. Yet none of us does, or can, exist in isolation, not even on the simplest levels like providing our daily food, the clothes we wear, the books we read. We are all very dependent on the flick of a switch, the turn of a knob; on the exchange of cash and services, on accumulated knowledge, on shared ideas. We are part of a chain, an army if you like. I prefer to think of it as a family – the family of the human race, created by God in his image.

We all need each other; we all depend on one another. It is rather like a jigsaw puzzle, where each piece is important in its own right, the uninteresting and difficult pieces of sky as much as the brilliant central pieces and the four corners. Leave one piece out, and the whole picture is marred because it is incomplete.

The bustling Radio Two studio in London, the local radio station in a northern city, or that lonely box in Goole, all remind me that I am a part of a wonderful world of people working together, sharing together, so that each person has the chance to be truly themselves. I get through each day, with its changing kaleidoscope of experiences, 'with a little help from my friends'.

God bless them, every one!

The man who fears the Lord keeps his friendships in repair,
for he treats his neighbour as himself.
(Ecclesiasticus 6.17, NEB)

*Thank you, Lord, that you have made me part of a family
    here on earth.*
*Keep me mindful of that, when I am tempted to despair,
    or blinded by arrogance.*
*Help me to recognise the needs and the gifts of others,
    and to accept them gracefully.*

49
Stand up, will you?

On holiday abroad one year, we went on a trip to see a famous and very popular castle. Our guide gave us firm instructions on how to behave when we got there: 'You've got your tickets, so you are going to have to push through the queue of people waiting at the entrance. I know it isn't very British, but it is the only way you'll get through. It will be no use standing back, you will be trampled in the rush.'

She was right. We did have to push, and wave our tickets, and take a few rude comments; but if we hadn't taken her advice we would have been there yet! It is true that the British are still – in the main – fairly peaceable, given to standing in orderly lines, letting others push past. 'Live and let live' is our motto, or, 'Anything for a quiet life'. Maybe that is what is nice about us – but we do sometimes come over as a 'couldn't care less' lot, with no courage of our convictions.

I believe, though, that there are some things which we should stand up for, or make a push for. It is a matter of what our priorities are in life.

For me, one of the most important things in my life is my faith in Jesus Christ. In fact, he is the pivot of my life. There is a hymn which begins, 'Stand up, stand up for Jesus'. It has a good rousing tune and it is sung very cheerfully – but how often do we Christians really stand up for Jesus? We prefer to keep our faith to ourselves, saying 'It's a private thing,' – but really we are rather cowardly. We don't want to make a fuss, or get ourselves laughed at, or be thought difficult or different.

I have been shamed into making a stand on certain issues through seeing others stand up in far more difficult conditions than I am ever likely to encounter. Maybe, just maybe, someone else will see my small token stand and stand alongside me, too. And maybe, just maybe, others will have the courage to stand with us.

What do you believe in most passionately? What difference does it make in your life? Enough to make you stand up and stand out for your beliefs? It is worth thinking about, isn't it?

> Build up your strength in union with the Lord and by means of His mighty power. Put on all the armour that God gives you, so that you will be able to stand up against the Devil's evil tricks. (Ephesians 6.10–11 GNB)

> *Lord, give me the courage and the strength*
>   *to stand up for what I know to be right,*
>   *whatever it costs me.*
> *May my actions as well as my words*
>   *testify to your saving power.*

50
What's your excuse?

When I was a youngster, I was always getting into trouble for talking. It wasn't my fault, though. Other people egged me on – they made me do it.

I used to fall into the canal quite regularly, but it wasn't my fault. The banks were slippery, and the fish darted away too quickly, and my fishing net handle wasn't long enough, so I overbalanced – well, it wasn't my fault, was it?

When I started work I was always forgetting the messages I was supposed to deliver, but it wasn't my fault. They should have written them down, not expected me to remember them all by myself. And when I got home late, it wasn't my fault, because no one told me what time it was . . .

I always had a good excuse, whatever I did, because – it wasn't my fault. It was *them*, those rather shadowy figures who were intent on tripping me up, leading me astray, making me forget, and putting clocks out of my eye line. It was useful to have *them* to blame, because then I could shift responsibility away from myself, which left me in the clear; and I could go on in my own sweet way, wearing that cross between the aggrieved innocent look and chronic self-righteousness.

Even now that I am middle-aged, I still try it on from time to time. Things happen which are not my fault, and I blame *them*. Yes, those shadowy figures still lurk around, so I can hang the blame round their necks.

I expect you know *them* too. I'm pretty sure they make you do things you shouldn't, and make you forget the things you should remember. Sometimes we give them names, and that is even better; names give our excuses rather more credibility – we hope.

Listening one day to part of a broadcast parliamentary debate, and reading the reports of it later in the newspaper, I realised that my friends *them* are everywhere. The debate was on law and order. An MP was blaming *them* for the increasing lawlessness in this country. *They* hadn't given a moral lead. And *they* included teachers, broadcasters and politicians – from the other side of the House, of course. The Archbishops of Canterbury and York got blamed too. Why? They had failed to tell us what was right and what was wrong, so how could people be expected to know the difference?

All that took me right back to my childhood. I could hear myself saying the same words: 'It's not my fault, not mine . . .' But I've learned something over the years. In fact I knew it all along, but I didn't admit it. I knew what was right and what was wrong. I knew who was to blame for what I did, or didn't do – it was me.

Of course, we do have a great many problems in this country, I'm not denying that. There is a great deal of lawlessness, moral decay, lack of control, and it does seem to be getting worse – although that may be due to us looking back and only seeing the good old days, when the sun always shone and everybody loved one another. But the problems of today, as they have been down the ages, are caused by individuals – us. We are all to blame.

The Bible doesn't mince words. It says, '*All* have sinned, and fall short of the glory of God.' *All* of us have 'missed the mark' – and that means you and me alike. It is not a matter of offering excuses, but of offering ourselves to God, and asking him to forgive us and change us. Those two go together – most of us want to be forgiven, but we don't always want to change. We need God's help and strength to do that.

At the end of the day we shall all have to give an account of our life, so maybe today is not too soon to start thinking about it – and doing something about it, too.

If we say that we have no sin, we deceive ourselves, and there is no truth in us. But if we confess our sins to God, he will keep his promise and do what is right: he will forgive us our sins and purify us from all our

wrondoing. If we say that we have not sinned, we make
God out to be a liar, and his word is not in us. (1 John
1.8–10 GNB)

Forgive me, Father, for trying to pull the wool
over your eyes in pretending I have not sinned.
Forgive me for my pride and arrogance,
for thinking I could fool you.
Forgive me and cleanse me from all my sin,
and keep me ever mindful
of your holiness and your love.

51
Giving up

With the season of Lent fast approaching, I was talking with a friend about 'giving up'. I always try to give up something for Lent, I told him. I see it as part of a discipline in my Christian life. He disagreed, saying that for some years he had given up smoking for Lent, and then happily took it up again at Easter. A couple of years ago he decided that if he was giving up smoking, and felt it was right to do so, then it should be for good, and not just for Lent, and he had done this.

I could see my friend's point; but the things we may choose to give up are not necessarily bad things, but very ordinary things which, if we give them up, concentrate the mind, and hopefully the heart, on the season of Lent. Giving up has a practical use as well. The money saved can be given to a Lenten appeal. Or, if not something of cash value, like giving up a television programme or getting up an hour earlier each day, then the time saved can be given over to God – an hour to pray, to study a Lent book, to visit someone, to take on an extra job at church. There are many positive uses to 'giving up'.

Immediately after his baptism, when Jesus had received the great affirmation from his Father, 'You are my beloved Son', he was 'led up by the Spirit into the wilderness to be tempted by the devil' – pushed out into the desert to face up to all the implications and possibilities of his ministry, and to discover God's way forward for him. Here he was, ready and eager to get on with his ministry. He was on the spiritual starting block, ready for God's 'Go'; and instead of going out to help people he was forced into forty days of solitude in the awesome, awful wilderness. Open to attack, physical, mental and spiritual. Desperately hungry, thirsty, tired, at the mercy of the destructive powers of the desert and the wiles of the devil. At his weakest and most vulnerable, he was tempted to use his powers for his own satisfaction, to attract a following by spectacular acts, and to compromise what he knew to be his own personal calling. All these temptations he wrestled with, and the answers came back loud and clear: 'It is written . . . It is written . . . It is written . . .' The Word of God, his prime weapon against the devil.

I have been in the ministry, one way or another, for a good few years now. I have had many years of experience, of guiding others, and being able to say with a smile, 'I've heard it all before.' That is a very dangerous stage to be at. It is so easy to do things my own way, to think I know all the answers and, more dangerous still, to think I am beyond temptation's power. So for me, Lent is a time when I go into the 'wilderness'. Not a Cook's tour, or a Winter Break in the sun, but time to be spent alone, with my defences down – purposely so. An opportunity to use that time I have 'given up' to get away by myself, for a day, or even a few hours, often to a windswept part of the north-east coast. Temptations to forward my ministry through self-gratification, gimmicks or compromise are often lurking in the background; and they can, if I am not careful and watchful, find a back door into my life and before I know it, take up residence. I need time to fight and pray, to take up the Word of God, and go on the attack. Lent gives me the chance, and the incentive, to do so.

The north-east wind on the Yorkshire coast in February and March is pretty piercing – it is described as 'a lazy wind, it doesn't go round you, it goes through you!' I find it helps to blow my cobwebs away in more ways than one. A mental 'spring clean' restores my cutting edge, and sharpens my desire for more of the living bread of Jesus.

So giving up a pleasurable programme or two, getting my work done earlier so I can get on to the wilderness, pays dividends. After all, if Jesus needed forty days and nights, a few hours each week of Lent won't do me any harm at all. In fact it does me a world of good, as through it I find the means to an even more joyful Eastertide!

The Spirit immediately drove him out into the wilderness. And he was in the wilderness forty days, tempted by Satan; and he was with the wild beasts; and the angels ministered to him. (Mark 1.12–13 RSV)

Lord Jesus Christ,
You endured forty days and forty nights in the desert.
You were tempted, but you won the victory.
Give me courage to venture into the wilderness,
*   to endure temptation,*
*   to know your victory in my life*
and to be strengthened to serve you
in the power of your Spirit.

52
Public image – private person

I was arranging a series of meetings to be held in York, and
was delighted when we were offered the chance of including
an overseas bishop as one of the speakers. He was to be in this
country on a preaching tour, and was available on the date of
our meeting. All who had heard him previously enthused
about his dynamic personality. He was a powerful preacher,
an exuberant character, full of joy and confidence in the
Lord. The more I heard, the more excited I got. 'Just what
we need, to stir us up and get us going,' I thought.

The man I met on the day was subdued and tired, not at all
what I had expected. At first I could get little response from
him. The reason was revealed by his host, who brought him
over to us. The bishop had recently been bereaved; his wife
had died, and although he had decided to continue with his
engagements, he was finding it very hard indeed. It was
almost impossible for him to speak or think about anything
but his loneliness and sadness.

I took the bishop into a quiet room and sat with him. We
talked, and I tried to show him that we understood, we
realised just how hard it was for him. It was obvious that he
was in a state of depression: he was full of grief and still in
shock. Then several of us prayed for him, and gently com-
forted him and encouraged him to share what was on his
heart. We gave him space and time, and made some altera-
tions to the style of meetings for the day. We tried to take the
pressure off him by allowing him to speak of his current
position, rather than 'fly the flag' for his diocese. Surrounded
with sympathetic loving care, he responded to us and began
to show something of his real personality, his deep Christian
convictions. There were even flashes of humour.

The meetings that day turned out rather differently from
those we had originally planned, but what came out was far

more important, both for the bishop and for us. I felt desperately sad for him, though, having to go on addressing meetings, preaching, enthusing others, with everybody expecting him to be full of energy and cheerfulness, when what he really needed was time to grieve, to be given love and support and space.

The bishop was not the first person, nor the last, to be put in the situation of having to give out when what was needed was the chance to receive from others. It happens so often, especially with people who are in the public eye and come with a 'reputation', people who hold high office. They are expected to perform all the time, never to put a foot wrong, and always to be on top form. It is easy to forget that they are people, and people with needs as well as gifts to share.

All of us are human, whatever our job or title or reputation. We are all made of flesh and blood, and subject to the stresses and strains of living in the world; to personal problems and tensions which affect body, mind and spirit. I am very fortunate, in that by nature I am a fairly easy-going extrovert, blessed with a rugged sort of constitution which stands up to pressures very well, with an inbuilt protective system and the ability to enjoy life to the full. Yet there are times when the last thing I want to do is open my mouth in public, address one more meeting, write yet another script, or do any of the thousand and one things I am thought to be able to do at the drop of a hat. One lady wrote to me, asking me to come at very short notice to speak at a conference: 'I know it's a long way and you are very busy, but words come so easily to you.' I felt like replying in words that came easily to mind, but would not have been at all polite. I didn't, of course!

We all think that the grass is greener on the other side of the street, and that the person on that other side can cope more easily than we can; that they are somehow different from us, and have a superhuman element that can be turned on and off as required. Then, when someone cracks under the strain, or does not come up to expectation, we are surprised and disappointed. We did not think it conceivable that they could be anything but one hundred per cent successful.

I shall always remember the visit of that African bishop, as I am sure will everyone who met him in York that day, with love and great affection. During his time with us we communicated heart to heart; and that was far more important than any casual and fleeting encounter with a visiting speaker could ever have been, however brilliant, dynamic or exuberant he might be. I hope we helped him carry his burden a little that day, and in some way gave him a chance to regain his strength by sharing his load. I believe God sent him to us to teach us a lesson we needed to learn; something that transcended the nuts and bolts of life in a diocese in Africa. It was a lesson about real partnership, with real people. I pray we learned it, and will remember it and act on it.

Bear one another's burdens, and so fulfil the law of Christ. (Galatians 6.2 RSV)

Lord,
Other people seem to be brighter and stronger than me.
They can cope with life more easily than I can;
they have confidence and power;
they always know what to say and do.
But I don't know their weaknesses, their sorrows,
the burdens they may be carrying.
Help me to recognise their needs,
and do my part in relieving them,
for your sake and in your strength.

Index of Bible references